Brazil

Brazil

Ann Heinrichs

Enchantment of the World
Second Series

Children's Press®

A Division of Grolier Publishing

NEW YORK   LONDON   HONG KONG   SYDNEY
DANBURY, CONNECTICUT

Consultant: Alexandre Diniz, M.A.

Please note: All statistics are as up-to-date as possible at the time of publication.

Library of Congress Cataloging-in-Publication Data

Heinrichs, Ann.
        Brazil / by Ann Heinrichs.
        p. cm. — (Enchantment of the world. Second series)
        Includes bibliographical references and index.
Summary: Describes the geography, plants, animals, history, economy, culture, and
        people of Brazil.
        ISBN 0-516-20602-8
        1. Brazil—Juvenile literature. [1. Brazil.] I. Title. II. Series
        F2508.5.H45 1997b
        918.1—dc21   97-14376
                                              CIP
                                              AC

To the memory of Chico Mendes
and Carmen Miranda

Contents

Cover photo:
Unloading fruit of
the asai palm from
boats at Belém

A Brazilian jungle

Sandy cliffs in Ceará, Brazil

Keeping the Fires Alive

Ten-year-old Taki takes careful aim with his bow and arrow. It is his first hunting expedition with the men. They left camp at daybreak, their ears trained to the barking sounds in the high forest canopy.

Taki releases the arrow and hits his mark. As the raccoon-like coati drops through the foliage, the men cheer for the young marksman. Their families will eat well today. Taki's father weaves palm leaves into a backpack to carry the boy's prize.

8

BACK AT THE CAMPSITE, WOMEN FAN the coals to start up a blaze. Taki's father is the fire keeper. When the group moves to a new hunting ground, he carries the last glowing embers to start the new fire. Taki's grandfather says they have kept the fire alive since their first ancestors walked the forest.

Taki's mother scrapes the reddish hairs off the coati and places it on the fire. Meanwhile, Taki helps with the men's chores. They repair the feathers on their arrows and sharpen the points. For practice, they take turns shooting at a log. A baby monkey, the community pet, scampers onto Taki's shoulder. It will stay with the group until it's grown and returns to the wild. Taki's grandfather says they must care for the offspring of animals killed in the hunt.

Taki and his friends take off into the jungle. They scramble up trees and swing on liana vines, landing with a splash in the river. One boy digs a hole in the mud on the riverbank. In a few minutes, it fills with water. Taki takes a leaf, curls it into

The coati is a relative of the raccoon.

a cone-shaped cup, and dips it in for a drink. The river water is muddy, but this water is clear and clean.

At the foot of a banana tree, Taki coils palm leaves into a thick rope and twists it around his feet. He binds them together—a tree trunk's width apart. Then he shuttles up the tree, knocks clusters of fruit to the ground, and shuttles back down.

The smell of roasting coati brings the boys back to camp. Taki, the honored hunter, gets the first juicy morsels. After eating meat, bananas, roots, and nuts, everyone is full.

By now it's early afternoon, the hottest part of the day. Taki stretches out in a hammock, his monkey nestled on his bare

In the Amazon, monkeys are often treated as pets.

Geopolitical map
of Brazil

A young Yanomami boy makes a bow out of a branch and vine.

chest. He drifts to sleep amid the screeches of birds, the rasp of insects, and a distant buzzing sound.

Taki has no idea that he's a Brazilian. He cannot imagine that, hundreds of miles away, other Brazilian children are working and playing in very different ways.

In other parts of the country, a child kicks a soccer ball across a dirt lot. Another tumbles through a martial arts routine. One boy swings a machete in a sugarcane field, while another gallops his horse across the high plains. One picks through a garbage can, while another races his dog along the beach.

Taki has never seen a soccer ball, or a horse, or a dog. He is one of the Guajá people of the northern Amazon. Recently, the Guajá have begun to notice a white tribe that lives nearby. Taki has heard their buzzing sounds—their motorboats and chainsaws.

One day soon, a man from the white tribe will come to the Guajá's hunting grounds. He will study their habits and mark off the limits of their land. After years of government procedures, the Guajá will be officially protected. They will have the right to do the things they have always done.

But this will probably not stop the buzzing. The men with the chainsaws will come closer and closer. Like termites, they will eat away at the forest. Next will come the fires.

Some Guajá will move deeper into the jungle. Others will learn to wear T-shirts and shorts and shoes. They will drink soda pop instead of river water and strike matches for fire.

But Taki knows none of this on this lazy afternoon. As the hammock gently sways, he is lost in private dreams. Tomorrow the families will move beyond the river. His father will carry the fire. One day, Taki himself will keep the fire for his people. He will pass on his grandfather's stories. He will teach his children the forest ways, as the Guajá always have. As they always will.

Forests, Beaches, and Plains

A hawk soaring high over Brazil would see rain forest and desert, emerald grasslands and murky swamps, sparkling beaches, and even some frosty mountain peaks.

The diverse landscapes of Brazil cover almost half of the South American continent. It is the fifth-largest country in the world, after Russia, China, Canada, and the United States. In fact, the continental United States could fit inside of Brazil!

D IAMOND-SHAPED BRAZIL HAS ALMOST EXACTLY THE SAME north-to-south and east-to-west measurements. The eastern half of the country bulges out into the sea. Cape São Roque, on Brazil's northeast coast, is only 1,850 miles (2,977 km) from Africa.

The Atlantic Ocean laps against Brazil's sandy beaches and rocky coasts for almost 4,600 miles (7,403 km). On land, Brazil borders ten other South American countries. Only Ecuador and Chile do not share a border with Brazil.

Sandy cliffs in Ceará state, on the Atlantic coast

Geographical Features

Largest City: São Paulo

Highest Elevation: Pico da Neblina, 9,888 feet (3,014 m)

Longest River: Amazon River, 1,960 miles (3,154 km) within Brazil, 4,000 miles (6,437 km) overall

World's Largest Dam: Itaipú Dam on the Paraná River

Lowest Average Temperature: São Paulo, 60°F (16°C), in July

Highest Average Temperature: Manaus, 73°F (23°C), in January

Driest Location: Northeast interior, 10 inches (25 cm) average annual rainfall

Oldest City: São Vicente, founded in 1530

World's Largest Rain Forest: Amazon rain forest, over 2 million square miles (5.18 million sq km)

A tree in bloom in the Amazon rain forest

The Amazon Region

The Amazon rain forest covers most of northern Brazil. Through it flows the mighty Amazon River on its way to the Atlantic Ocean. In Brazil, the rain forest is called Amazônia.

Manaus and Belém are the largest cities in northern Brazil. Manaus is the country's major inland port. It is on the Rio Negro, a few miles from its juncture with the Amazon, and is the starting point for many expeditions into the Amazon region. In the 1890s, rubber barons built Manaus into the "Paris of the Jungle," even building a grand opera house there.

Belém, on the Atlantic at the Amazon's mouth, is the capital of Pará state. In the far north are the Guiana Highlands, whose peaks are shrouded in clouds. One of them is Pico da Neblina, Brazil's highest point.

Topographical map of Brazil

The Northeast

Northeastern Brazil juts out into the Atlantic Ocean. Beaches and farmland line the coast, but much of the interior is an arid plain. This is called the backlands, or the *sertão*. Some cattle ranches survive here, but the soil makes poor farmland. Droughts and floods are common, too. The interior is poorly developed, but its oil fields are an important resource. Almost 30 percent of the population lives in the northeast. Its major cities, Salvador and Recife (often called the "Venice of Brazil" because of its canals and bridges), are on the coast. The northeast was the first center of colonial Brazil. Much of the country's unique flavor—its music, food, and folklore—arose here.

The Central Plateau

South of the Amazon region is the *planalto*, or central plateau. Brasília, the capital, is a cluster of civilization in this sparsely populated area. Beyond the city, broad savannas—grassy plains—are scattered with scrubby trees.

Farther south are rolling hills, rich farmland, and luxurious grasslands. Much of this land is carved into huge cattle ranches and plantations, or *fazendas*. Some compete for land with the many Indian reserves in the west. The Mato Grosso swampland, or Pantanal, straddles the Paraguay River in west-central Brazil.

The Pantanal is one of the largest wildlife reserves in the world.

The Pantanal

The Pantanal, in western Mato Grosso state, is one of the largest wildlife reserves—and swamps—in the world. It covers about 100,000 square miles (259,000 sq km) and spills over into Paraguay and Bolivia. Capybaras, caimans (alligators), and giant anteaters thrive in this marshy habitat. One of the Pantanal's exotic water birds is the jabiru stork, which stands 5 feet (1.5 m) tall.

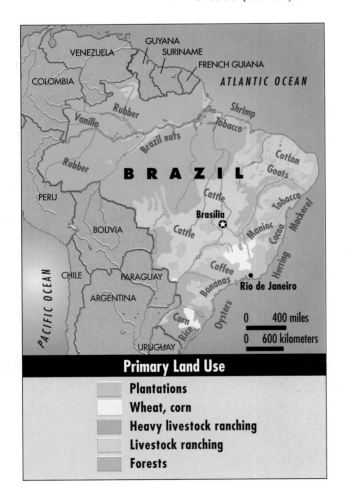

Primary Land Use

- Plantations
- Wheat, corn
- Heavy livestock ranching
- Livestock ranching
- Forests

The Industrial Heartland

The southeast is the most developed part of Brazil. It has the most fertile farms and pastures, the most productive mines, and almost half the population.

The Brazilian Highlands run north to south in this region. Their eastern face, the Great Escarpment, slopes up steeply from the narrow coastal strip. In the past, this mountain barrier blocked people from getting into the interior.

Huge plantations grow coffee and grain in the rich, red soil of São Paulo state. The areas around São Paulo and Rio de Janeiro, Brazil's largest cities, are highly industrialized. Belo Horizonte, the capital of Minas Gerais state, is

another center of industry. In colonial times, gold and dia-monds were mined in Minas Gerais. Now its iron-ore deposits are the basis for Brazil's steel industry.

Much of Brazil's steel comes from mines in Minas Gerais.

Gaúchos

Land of the Gaúchos

In southern Brazil, the highlands drop down to broad plains called the *pampas*. These are grazing lands for thousands of cattle. Gaúchos, Brazil's legendary cowboys, tend the herds on huge ranches there.

Porto Alegre is the capital of Rio Grande do Sul, Brazil's southernmost state. It was founded in 1742 by set-tlers from the Azores Islands. German and Italian immigrants followed in the 1800s. The landscape features vineyards, pastures, rocky coastlines,

Looking at Brazil's Cities

São Paulo (top) was founded by Jesuit priests in 1554. Coffee barons beautified it with mansions, parks, and museums. Today, São Paulo is Brazil's industrial and financial hub. The modern downtown area centers on the Praça da Sé, and the Avenida Paulista is the major financial street. São Paulo's many ethnic neighborhoods and restaurants reflect its international culture.

Rio de Janeiro, or simply "Rio," (top left) is a seafront city with granite peaks rising sharply behind it. Sugar Loaf Mountain, rising high above Guanabara Bay, can be seen from far out at sea. Another landmark, the 130-foot (40-m) statue of Christ the Redeemer (left), overlooks Rio from atop Corcovado ("Hunchback") Mountain. Rio combines excitement, natural beauty, culture, and fun. Both locals and foreigners are drawn to its dazzling white beaches, jungle-covered mountains, festivals, and museums.

Salvador (right), the capital of Bahia state, was divided into an upper and lower city in colonial times. Forts and docks lined the beaches. Behind them, homes and government buildings covered the hills. Beautifully decorated mansions, churches, and public squares remain from Salvador's "golden age" as the colony's busiest port. Brazil's African heritage is most visible in Salvador. African influence appears in spicy foods, candomblé religious ceremonies, and the martial art of capoeira.

and forested hills. Local industries include making wine and leather goods.

The major river in the south, the Paraná, forms part of the Brazil-Paraguay border. The two countries built a powerful hydroelectric power plant, Itaipú Dam, on the Paraná. Only a few miles away is spectacular Iguaçú Falls, spilling over the border into Argentina.

The Amazon River

Countless adventurers have lost their lives exploring the Amazon River. Starting at one end or the other, they were foiled by treacherous rapids, Indians, or starvation. The Spaniard Francisco de Orellana was the first to travel from its upper reaches to its mouth in 1541–1542. Today, ships can easily navigate the Amazon all the way to Iquitos, Peru.

From its source in the Andes Mountains, the Amazon courses across the continent for about 4,000 miles (6,437 km). It flows through Brazil for 1,960 miles (3,154 km) before reaching the sea. In some places, the Amazon has carved cliffs as deep as 300 feet (91 m). Near its mouth, the Amazon splits, creating a wide delta.

The Amazon is the second-longest river in the world, after Egypt's Nile River, but it ranks first in volume of water, number of branches, and drainage area. One-fifth of the freshwater that enters the world's oceans flows from the mouth of the Amazon.

Over a thousand rivers and streams branch off from the Amazon. Seventeen of these tributaries are over 1,000 miles (1,609 km) long. The longest is the Madeira, running for

more than 2,000 miles (3,219 km). Another is the Rio Negro, which means "Black River." Its water gets its dark color from decomposing plants upstream. Other major tributaries are the Tapajós and Xingu Rivers.

More than half of Brazil is in the Amazon's drainage basin—the land whose rainwater ends up in the Amazon. The best soil in the Amazon Basin is on its floodplains. During the

Where the Rio Negro flows into the Amazon River, near Manaus, the Rio Negro's dark water mixes dramatically with that of the Amazon.

Facts about the Amazon River

Origin of Name:
The name *Amazon* comes from Greek mythology. Huge, wild women called Amazons were believed to live in what is now Brazil.

Length: 4,000 miles (6,437 km)

Volume: 20 percent of the freshwater that flows into world's oceans

Area Drained: 2.3 million square miles (6 million sq km)

Also in Drainage Basin: Peru, Ecuador, Bolivia, Venezuela

Number of Tributaries: over 1,000; more than 200 in Brazil

Discharge at Mouth: 7 million cubic feet (198,219 cu m) per second

Major Inland Port: Manaus

Number of Bridges: None

rainy season, the rivers flood, leaving mineral-rich silt behind. When the floodwaters are high, parts of the Amazon River are several miles wide. Some early explorers thought the river was a vast inland sea.

Iguaçú Falls

The São Francisco is Brazil's second-largest river, measuring 1,988 miles (3,200 km). It rises in southern Minas Gerais, flows east and north, and empties into the Atlantic. In the south, the Paranaíba and Rio Grande join to form the Paraná. It flows south into Argentina's Río de la Plata.

Iguaçú Falls

Iguaçú Falls plunges through a gorge across the Brazil-Argentina border. Around the horseshoe-shaped rim are 275 falls, separated by rocks and islands. Garganta do Diabo, or "Devil's Throat," is the most violent drop. From rim to rim, the waterfall measures about 2.5 miles (4 km) wide. From top to bottom, it plunges 300 feet (91 m), sending up walls of foam and spray. About 1.2 million gallons (4.5 million l) of water cascade over the edge every second.

Visitors to Iguaçú Falls can follow trails along the bank for a spectacular overall view. More adventurous types choose to walk on the *passarelas*. These shaky, wooden catwalks teeter on the edge of the roaring falls. The experience is its own reward—hearing the close-up sound of the thundering water and watching rainbows appear in the spray.

The Perfect Climate?

Brazil's climate ranges from warm to hot all year long. It never gets really cold. Visitors and locals alike swear that Brazil has the perfect climate.

Most of Brazil lies south of the equator, so its seasons are the opposite of those in the Northern Hemisphere. June, July, and August are the winter months, while summer comes in December, January, and February.

The hottest areas are those nearest to the equator, which cuts across the northern tip of Brazil. In Manaus, which is only about 200 miles (322 km) from the equator, the average high temperature in September and October—springtime—is 92°F (33°C).

The northern rain forest is hot and humid, while the northeast and the central plateau are hot and dry. The average temperature in the Amazon Basin is 81°F (27°C). But the northeast interior is even hotter, often hitting 100°F (38°C).

On the southern plateaus, farther from the equator, the climate is warm and dry. Winters can even be cool. In July (winter), São Paulo's average temperature dips down to 60°F (16°C). In the hot summer month of January, it averages about 73°F (23°C).

On the lower Amazon River floodplain, the floodwaters leave behind mineral-rich silt.

True to its name, the rain forest is wet. Most of the Amazon's rain falls between January and June. The western Amazon region can get more than 160 inches (406 cm) of rain a year, which averages out to almost ½ inch (1.2 cm) every day of the year! Compare this to New York City's annual rainfall of 42 inches (107 cm). The Amazon is almost four times as wet.

In contrast, the parched interior of the northeast is the driest region. In some places, the annual rainfall is only 10 inches (25 cm).

In the central and southern plateaus, about 50 inches (127 cm) of rain fall each year, mainly in the summer months, from November through May. Mountains in the south actually get frost and snow sometimes, but it melts quickly.

Wild Things

Forests cover half of Brazil, and most are in the hot, humid Amazon region. Here, the topmost branches form a canopy, or leafy ceiling, high above the forest floor. Frisky monkeys and brilliantly colored birds dart among the branches, while millions of creatures scurry around far below. This lush, tropical jungle is the largest rain forest in the world.

Towering broadleaf evergreens form the top layer of the forest. Their upper branches spread out and tangle together. Thick vines curl around the trunks and dangle from the limbs. Shorter tree species form the lower layers of greenery. The foliage is so thick that very little light reaches the ground. Even at midday, people may need lanterns to find their way through the shadows.

There are more tree species in the Amazon rain forest than anywhere else on the planet. As many as 3,000 species have been found in 1 square mile (2.6 sq km). Palm, banana, mahogany, and rubber trees are some of the best-known varieties.

One of the giants of the rain forest is the Brazil nut tree. It can grow higher than 150 feet (46 m), with a trunk 15 feet (4.6 m) wide. At the crown, its branches arch like an umbrella. The "nuts" are really seeds encased in heavy pods. If a falling pod lands on someone's head, it can

Brazil nuts in the pod

cause serious injury or even death. Brazil nuts are an excellent dietary source of the mineral selenium, which may help prevent ovarian cancer.

Rain forest trees are "gardens" for other plants. Their trunks and limbs are covered with mosses, lichens, orchids, philodendrons, and ferns. These plants sink their roots into the rotting leaves and animal droppings that build up on the trees. (Plants that anchor themselves to a tree but do not draw nutrients from it are called epiphytes.)

Indians and Rubber

Amazon Indians were the first people to process rubber. They cut V-shaped slashes in the trees and collected the white liquid, or latex, that oozed out. They used the latex as an insect repellent or as a waterproof covering for their beautiful feathered robes. When heated over a fire, the latex thickened into raw rubber. The Indians then formed the rubber into balls, bottles, and footwear.

These orchids grow on tree trunks in the rain forest.

Beasts Above and Below

Jungle animals are most active—and make the most noise—between sunrise and midmorning. As the day gets hotter, they settle down, conserve their energy, and nap. When the sun drops low in the sky, they start up their ruckus again.

Tropical birds are the most colorful creatures in the high canopy. Red, blue, and green parrots, scarlet macaws, and toucans with banana-sized beaks live in the topmost branches. Some of the smaller birds are parakeets, flycatchers, and swifts. Hawks and vultures soar overhead, while long-legged herons, ibises, and storks wade along rivers and swamps.

Howler monkeys are the largest primates in the Amazon (other than humans). They get their name from their raucous barking and hooting sounds. Gibbons, capuchins, spider monkeys, and squirrel monkeys are some of the howler's cousins.

Opposite: **The toucan is one of the most colorful tropical birds in the Amazon.**

Three-toed sloths spend most of their time hanging upside down with their hooklike claws. They eat, sleep, and even have their babies in this position. Moths, beetles, and algae live in the sloth's fur. Opossums are "hangers," too. They sleep hanging by their tail all day and forage for fruit and insects at night. The coati feeds in the daytime, unlike its raccoon relatives.

Clinging to a tree, a male three-toed sloth munches on a leaf.

Giant Rodent!

Rats, mice, hamsters, and guinea pigs are familiar North American rodents. The Amazon's capybara is the world's largest rodent, weighing over 100 pounds (45 kg). It stands as tall as a German shepherd dog and looks like a very large guinea pig or a small hippopotamus. Capybaras even have their own home page on the Internet!

Down on the ground, there are piglike peccaries and tapirs, chunky capybaras, and giant anteaters with big, bushy tails. Any of these might make a meal for a jaguar or a black panther. The jaguar is now one of the Amazon's many endangered species. Poachers (illegal hunters) make their living by selling the high-priced skins.

The *jacaré*, or caiman, is a relative of the alligator. Black caimans are becoming rare because they, too, are hunted for their skins. Poachers hunt them at night, scanning the riverbanks with a flashlight until they see a caiman's shining pair of eyes.

Over 200 species of snake live in the Amazon. Boa constrictors and anacondas are the largest. Anacondas are the subject of many terrifying Indian legends. They swallow their prey whole and grow as long as 40 feet (12 m)—the height of a four-story building!

The caiman is related to the alligator.

Leafcutter Ladies

With their saw-toothed jaws, leafcutter ants cut leaves into pieces small enough to carry. In long caravans, they march the leaf fragments back to their underground colony. There they chew the leaves into a mulch to grow the fungus that is their only food. All the workers are females. The males only provide sperm to fertilize the queen ant's eggs.

Farmers at the forest's edge often find their fence posts shredded by termites, but termites are good for the forest. They add to the nutrients in the soil by eating away at dead trees.

Fish and Other Water Creatures

The Amazon's *pirarucú*, also called the paiche, is the world's largest freshwater fish. Some are 10 feet (3 m) long and weigh 250 pounds (113 kg), but even larger specimens have been reported. The pirarucú is a fruit-eater. It springs out of the water to nip fruits from overhanging tree branches. Indians use its tough scales and bony tongue as tools. Another Amazon fish, the *tambaqui*, can crack nuts in its teeth.

People in the Amazon region are not afraid of piranhas and their powerful, razor-toothed jaws. They're just very careful. Although piranhas are meat-eaters, they attack humans only when their natural food supplies are low. On the other hand, the Amazon's giant, bloodsucking leeches latch on to a human host at every opportunity.

Most dolphins are saltwater creatures that live in the ocean. However, a pink dolphin lives in the Amazon River. According to an Indian legend, it changes into a human at night and roams the land.

Many of the Amazon's fish are edible. They are sold in the fish markets of Manaus and Belém, along with shrimp, crabs, oysters, eels, stingrays, and turtles. Heavy fishing is taking its toll, though. Fishermen have to travel several days upriver from Manaus to find good fishing grounds.

Piranhas have razor-toothed jaws.

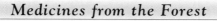

Medicines from the Forest

One-quarter of the world's medicines come from the rain forest. They are based on extracts from leaves, bark, and even insects. Indians have used these healing substances for thousands of years. They know which ones to use for snakebites, insect bites, cuts, burns, and countless other problems.

Many ethnobotanists—scientists who study beliefs and traditions related to plants—are studying medicinal plants in the rain forest today. They learn their uses from the Indians, collect samples, and analyze their chemical makeup. The next step is to duplicate these substances in the laboratory so they can be made into medicines that could help millions of people.

Plant Life Beyond the Amazon

Toward the east coast, where there is less rainfall, the trees are not as tall as rain forest species. Many lose their leaves during the dry season. Because this semideciduous forest is easier to clear than the rain forest, the first colonists settled here. Indians showed them how to eat the tangy, pear-shaped fruit of the cashew tree. Hanging at the bottom of each fruit was a bonus—a savory nut.

A thorny shrub called *caatinga* infests the dry northeastern backlands. Farther south, in central Brazil, is the *cerrado*, a woodland savanna with hardy grasses and scrubby trees. More luxuriant grasslands cover the southeastern plateau.

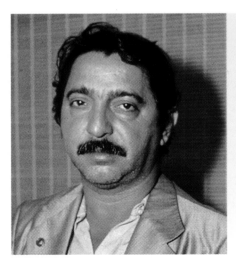

Chico Mendes: Activist and Labor Leader

Francisco Mendes Filho (1944–1988), known as Chico Mendes, was born in Xapuri in far-western Acre state. He was a rain forest activist and the leader of the rubber-tappers' union. Mendes organized heroic protests against those who were destroying forestland. He was murdered in 1988 by a disgruntled rancher.

Flowering bushes and trees add brilliant splashes of color to the southern highlands. Araucaria trees, or Paraná pines, grow there, too. These pine forests are quickly disappearing as they are cut for construction timber.

Much of the Amazon rain forest has been burned to clear the land for cattle ranching and farming.

Vanishing Forests

Day by day, the Amazon rain forest is shrinking. Loggers, miners, ranchers, and farmers destroy thousands of trees every day.

In the 1970s, mining and logging companies began pushing into the forest. Farmers and ranchers moved in, too. Drought in the northeast was unusually severe, and thousands of landless peasants had nowhere to go. Government-sponsored programs made it easy for them to settle in the forest and claim rights to the land. Day and night, fires raged through the forest to make way for farms and ranches.

By 1988, the forest was disappearing at the rate of 8,300 square miles (21,500 sq km) a year. All over the world, environmentalists were in an uproar. They warned that the entire planet depends on the rain forests for oxygen. Once an area is cleared, it takes 300 years to grow back to its former state.

Under pressure from the world community, Brazil began aggressive conservation programs. In the early 1990s, deforestation was down to about 4,250 square miles (11,000 sq km) a year.

In 1992, Brazil hosted the United Nations Conference on Environment and Development, called the Earth Summit. Participants pledged to protect the tropical rain forests of the world. The international attention also led Brazilian officials to set aside and protect Yanomami Indian lands.

In the Amazon region today, there are twenty-four national forests, eight national parks, seven biological reserves, three

The Amazon and the Greenhouse Effect

The Amazon rain forest protects the entire planet. When fuels such as petroleum are burned, they release carbon dioxide into the atmosphere. This layer of gas surrounds the globe, trapping the sun's heat—just as a greenhouse traps warm air inside. Scientists call this the "greenhouse effect."

Rain forest plants take in huge amounts of carbon dioxide to use in photosynthesis. One hectare (2.5 acres) of the Amazon rain forest absorbs one ton of carbon dioxide a year. But carbon dioxide levels around the world keep rising. Today, the atmosphere contains 30 percent more carbon dioxide than it did in 1900.

Scientists estimate that destroying the Amazon would raise the Earth's temperature 5 degrees Fahrenheit (3 degrees Celsius). The added warmth would melt the polar ice caps enough to raise ocean levels far into coastal lands.

ecological reserves, and many other protected areas. Strict regulations control economic activities in the rain forest. Loggers are required to plant new trees wherever they cut. Roads and power plants must be built in ways that preserve the environment. Several countries are working with Brazil to monitor the rain forest through satellite pictures.

However, illegal cutting and burning continue. The forest is too big to police, and everyone knows it. There are many ways to get around the laws. Besides, local politicians hate to give up their own region's development in favor of conservation. The national government is committed to an ideal that may take many years to achieve. It hopes to find a perfect balance through "sustainable development"—using the forest's resources without destroying the forest.

Recent regulations require loggers to "reforest"—to renew the forest cover by planting young trees.

Once Upon a Time in Brazil

Millions of years ago, South America was joined to the continent of Africa. If you compare Brazil's coastline to the west coast of Africa, you can see how they once fit together. Eastern Brazil's "bulge" fits right under the "hump" of West Africa. About 400 million years ago, the two landmasses split and began to drift apart.

PEOPLE FROM SIBERIA STARTED MIGRATING INTO NORTH America around 15,000 years ago. Most scholars believe they crossed a land bridge, where Alaska's Bering Strait is now. In time, people migrated down through North America into Central and South America. Brazil's Indians are direct descendants of those early migrants.

Around 11,000 years ago, one group of these Indians lived in a cave at Monte Alegre in the Brazilian Amazon. Remains found in the cave show that the people ate tropical fruits, fish, shellfish, and large animals. They used tools such as stone spear-points and knives. Later residents in the area organized fishing villages and, still later, farming communities.

Most Indians were seminomads who hunted, fished, and gathered wild plants. Some lived in villages with up to 5,000 residents. For many, the main source of carbohydrates was a root called manioc, or cassava. Manioc is still a common food in Brazil today.

The root of the manioc, or cassava plant, is a staple Amazon crop that dates back to the time of the early Indians.

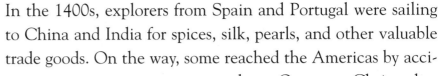
Christopher Columbus watching for land on his voyage to the Americas

In the 1400s, explorers from Spain and Portugal were sailing to China and India for spices, silk, pearls, and other valuable trade goods. On the way, some reached the Americas by accident. One was Christopher Columbus. He landed on an island a few hundred miles from Brazil. Thinking he had reached the Indies in Asia, he called the people "Indians."

Soon Spain and Portugal were in a race to snap up this "New World." Pope Alexander VI, head of the Roman Catholic Church, stepped in. He took a map and drew a line through the New World, from north to south. This was called the Line of Demarcation. All lands west of the line would belong to Spain. Those to the east—including eastern Brazil—would be Portugal's. The two countries agreed to this division in the 1494 Treaty of Tordesillas.

Cabral's Voyage

Pedro Álvares Cabral (1467/68–1520) set sail from Portugal in 1500, headed for India. No one knows why his ships veered toward the southwest on their Atlantic voyage. Cabral knew very well that the route to India was southeast, around the tip of Africa. Nevertheless, on April 22, he spotted the coast of Brazil and landed at what is now Pôrto Seguro. Cabral had no idea where he was, but he claimed the region for Portugal anyway, naming the land *Terra da Vera Cruz* ("Land of the True Cross"). He sailed on, leaving two crewmen behind to carry on explorations. They were never heard from again.

Cabral taking possession of Brazil

There may have been as many as 5 million Indians in Brazil when Cabral arrived. Those he met along the coast were the Tupinambá. Notes from Cabral's voyage say they wore no clothes but adorned themselves with tattoos and colorful feathers. They lived in huts, sailed on rafts, and played musical instruments.

Cabral's newfound land became a Portuguese colony, and Portuguese settlers began to move in.

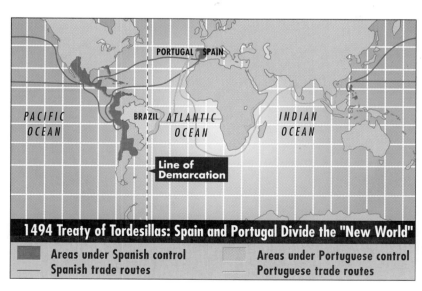

PORTUGAL SPAIN

PACIFIC OCEAN

BRAZIL ATLANTIC OCEAN

INDIAN OCEAN

Line of Demarcation

1494 Treaty of Tordesillas: Spain and Portugal Divide the "New World"

Areas under Spanish control
Spanish trade routes

Areas under Portuguese control
Portuguese trade routes

Once Upon a Time in Brazil **47**

As they hacked their way through the forests, they found a tree whose bark made a brilliant red dye. Some said the red tree trunks shimmered like glowing coals in a fire. They called the tree *pau-brasil* ("blazing wood"), or brazilwood. This gave the colony its name, and brazilwood became Brazil's first export.

Plantations and Cities

The colonists found a warm climate and rich soil in the coastal strip of northeastern Brazil. They planted sugarcane on large plantations and shipped sugar back to Europe. Their earliest settlements were Salvador and Recife, and Salvador became the colonial capital.

The Portuguese raided the forests, rounding up Indians to work the fields. But the Indians fought back or ran deeper into the jungle. Many were killed, and entire tribes died of diseases

they caught from the settlers. Catholic missionaries tried to protect the Indians from slave raids, but they were not very successful.

The colonists shipped in slaves from West Africa as a fresh labor supply. Intermarriage among the Portuguese, Indians, and Africans was common. In time, the mix of races, languages, and customs produced a unique Brazilian culture.

Coffee has long been a profitable product for Brazilian farmers. Here, workers spread coffee berries to ferment and dry.

Treasures of the South

In the south, colonists founded the cities of São Vicente and São Paulo. From the coast they pushed inland, clearing paths through the thick forests. Their discoveries—of gold in 1695 and diamonds in 1729—brought a rush of Portuguese fortune-hunters who opened mines in the state of Minas Gerais.

Plantations in the south grew a new "boom" crop—coffee. The southern soil favored cotton, too. Cattle ranches sprang up to feed the mining centers. Rio de Janeiro, perched on a point on the Atlantic, had the best harbor for shipping out gold and other Brazilian goods. In 1763, Rio de Janeiro became the colony's new capital.

By this time, Portuguese settlers had pushed far beyond the Line of Demarcation and into Spain's territory. In 1777, Portugal and Spain signed the Treaty of San Ildefonso, which set Brazil's borders roughly where they are today.

Opposite: **The earliest colonists planted sugarcane in Recife. This plantation just north of Recife still yields sugar.**

Once Upon a Time in Brazil **49**

Tiradentes: Dentist and Patriot

Tiradentes (1748–1792), or "Tooth Puller," was a dentist who led Brazil's first uprising for independence in 1789. Born Joaquim Jose da Silva Xavier, Tiradentes was inspired by successful independence movements in France and the United States. For leading a rebellion in Minas Gerais, Tiradentes was tried and hanged. His execution day, April 21, is now a national holiday.

The Kingdom of Portugal and Brazil

France invaded Portugal in 1807. Dom João of Portugal took the royal family and fled to Rio de Janeiro for safety. In 1815, João named his empire the Kingdom of Portugal and Brazil.

João made many changes in Brazil. For the first time, foreigners were allowed to own land. Factories were built and foreign traders came in. In spite of these improvements, however, many Brazilians wanted to be free of Portuguese rule. They got their chance in 1821 when João was called back to Portugal. He left his son Pedro in charge.

Brazil's First Emperor and Empress

Pedro I (1798–1834) led Brazilians to independence and became Brazil's first emperor. In a war with Argentina, Pedro lost a Brazilian province that became Uruguay. Also, citizens resented him for placing Portuguese people in high government positions. Pedro was forced to abdicate the throne after nine years as emperor.

Maria Leopoldina (1797–1826), wife of Pedro I, was Brazil's first empress. Born an archduchess of Austria, she married Pedro by proxy (long-distance, through representatives). She loved Brazil's natural beauty and urged Pedro to make Brazil independent. A neighborhood in Rio de Janeiro and a samba school are named after her.

Pedro was in love with the idea of independence. One day, a Portuguese messenger brought Pedro orders to leave Brazil. As legend has it, Pedro whipped out his sword and cried, "Independence or death!" Brazil declared its independence in 1822, and Pedro was named Emperor Pedro I. In 1831, he gave up the throne and returned to Portugal, leaving behind his five-year-old son. When the boy was only fifteen years old, he began his rule as Emperor Pedro II.

During his forty-nine-year reign, Pedro II brought Brazil into the modern world. He started a public school system and built factories to make cotton into cloth. Roads and railroads penetrated the interior, and steamships chugged up the Amazon.

Pedro II, who became emperor of Brazil in 1840, ruled for forty-nine years.

Shiploads of European settlers poured in to make their fortune. Many grew coffee in the rich, red soil around São Paulo. Brazil became the foremost coffee producer in the world. Gold mines flourished in the interior, and a new rubber industry sprang up in the Amazon. Brazil was now exporting coffee, rubber, cacao (cocoa), and cattle.

Timeline of Royal Succession

1808	Arrival of Dom João from Portugal
1822	Accession of Dom Pedro I
1840	Reign of Pedro II, Dom Pedro's son
1889	Rule of Pedro II ends; Brazil is declared a republic.

The Birth of the Republic

Brazil, the last nation in the Western Hemisphere to abolish slavery, had imported more African slaves than any other country in the world. When Pedro II outlawed slavery in 1888, the powerful plantation owners were enraged. With the army's help, they forced Pedro out of the country. On November 15, 1889, Brazil was declared a republic. General Manoel Deodoro da Fonseca, who had led the struggle, became the nation's first president.

The new republic attracted more immigrants than ever before. German, Italian, and Japanese workers poured in to work Brazil's farms and mines in place of the slaves. Some companies even placed ads in foreign newspapers to lure more workers in.

Brazil had a rough time in the early 1900s when Southeast Asia became the world's biggest rubber supplier. The nation's rubber industry crashed as quickly as it had risen. Coffee took its place, soon making up 70 percent of Brazil's entire exports. But when world coffee prices dropped, the

A principal business street in Rio at the turn of the century

whole country suffered. Amid the chaos, army officers and powerful dictators sometimes took over.

During World War I (1914–1918), industrial countries were busy manufacturing war supplies. This gave Brazil a chance to fill the gap. Factories sped up production, supplying consumer goods to both Brazilian and foreign markets.

The Coffee-and-Milk Republic

Coffee-growing São Paulo and milk-producing Minas Gerais had become Brazil's dominant states. As an unwritten rule, the presidency alternated between candidates from these two regions. This arrangement was known as the *República do Café com Leite*, or the "Coffee-and-Milk Republic."

In 1930, the outgoing president from São Paulo insisted that another São Paulo candidate be his successor. When he broke the pattern, it destroyed the republic. Army officers from Minas Gerais banded together with people from other states and took over the government. They made Getúlio Vargas president.

The Vargas Era

Vargas turned out to be a good president in many ways. He allowed trade unions, so that workers had shorter hours and higher wages. He also expanded voting rights to all adults, including—for the first time—women.

The Great Depression of the 1930s hit Brazil hard, just as it did other countries. Businesses failed and millions of people were out of work. To Vargas, the situation called for emer-

President Getúlio Vargas, shown addressing political dignitaries in 1942, served as Brazil's president for a total of almost twenty years.

gency measures. He dissolved Congress, gave himself the powers of a dictator, and canceled many of the freedoms he had helped to create. Vargas used his powers to put people to work and help Brazil out of its slump. New schools, highways, and power plants were built. One project, a steel factory in Volta Redonda, became the biggest steel plant in Latin America.

World War II (1939–1945) gave the nation another boost. Again, Brazil's factories supplied the world with goods

The bustling city of São Paulo during Brazil's economic boom in the 1960s and 1970s

that other countries had stopped making. Steel, automobile, and chemical industries boomed. The military removed Vargas in 1945, and basic freedoms were put back in place.

The Economic Miracle and Military Rule

After the war, foreign companies began to move in and build factories. President Juscelino Kubitschek built roads, power plants, and, in 1960, the new capital city of Brasília. To make Brazil less dependent on imports, Kubitschek encouraged steel, automobile, shipbuilding, and machinery industries. The result was an "economic miracle." In the 1960s and 1970s, the nation exploded with prosperity.

However, the miracle did not work for everyone. Masses of rural people left their farms and swarmed into the industrial cities to find jobs. With no place to live, they set up ramshackle shantytowns on the outskirts of cities. Poverty and unemployment reached emergency levels.

Brazil in World War II

Brazil, like the United States and Canada, sided with the Allies in World War II. Brazil declared war on the Axis powers in 1942. The Brazilian Expeditionary Force of 25,000 troops fought in Italy.

Once Upon a Time in Brazil **55**

Fernando Cardoso at his inauguration as Brazil's thirty-eighth president in 1995

One after another, Brazil's presidents tried to deal with the growing problems. Wary of communist influences, the army took over the government in 1964. Military-backed dictators ruled for the next two decades. Fed up with corrupt officials, civilians took back the government in 1985.

Challenges to the New Democracy

The new democratic government faced staggering problems. To finance its progress, Brazil had borrowed heavily from foreign banks. Now it owed enormous debts. Prices were more than doubling every year. Worldwide, environmentalists pressured Brazil to stop clearing its rain forests. Yet Brazil badly needed to develop more land for exports to help pay its debts.

Only in the 1990s did the economy begin to get on an even keel. President Fernando Collor de Mello took office in 1990 and introduced sweeping reforms. He cut government spending and began transferring government-run industries to private companies. His successor, Itamar Franco, appointed Fernando Henrique Cardoso as minister of the economy. Cardoso's 1994 economic program included a new unit of money, the *real*. Within months, Brazil's runaway prices had settled down.

Coasting on his new popularity, Cardoso became president in 1995. He continued to remove industries from state control. Cardoso also worked to improve public schools, social conditions, and human rights in Brazil.

In 1995, Brazil entered a trade agreement with three of its South American neighbors—Argentina, Paraguay, and

Uruguay. Their union, called MERCOSUL (Mercado Commun do Sul) is similar to the European Union (EU). It removes import taxes among members, making for a free flow of trade goods.

Current Issues

Brazil is still expanding economically. It is exporting more goods than ever. Between the very rich and the very poor is a growing middle class. Still, many problems remain. Land developers and environmentalists are locked in eternal battles. Prices are still high, and the country is still deep in debt. Cities are plagued with poverty, unemployment, overcrowding, and crime. But Brazilians have a knack for surviving crises. Today, with the steady hand of a stable government, the future looks much brighter than the turbulent past.

How the Republic Works

Since the 1500s, Brazil has been a colony, a kingdom, an empire, and a republic. Today, Brazil's official name is the Federative Republic of Brazil.

Memories of the monarchy still live, though. As recently as 1993, Brazilians were asked to vote on whether they wanted to return to the monarchy and be ruled by a king. As it turned out, the vast majority opted to keep the republic.

BRAZIL'S 1891 CONSTITUTION CALLED FOR A FEDERAL government with three branches: executive, legislative, and judicial. Several constitutions have been in effect since then. The present constitution dates from October 5, 1988, and the three-way division of power remains.

The Executive

Brazil's president is the chief of state and heads the executive branch of government. Presidential powers are broad. If national security is at stake, the president may impose federal rule on a state.

Brazil's National Flag

Brazil's flag features a large yellow diamond on a green background. Green stands for Brazil's lush forests and fields. Yellow represents Brazil's rich deposits of gold. In the diamond is a blue circle with twenty-seven white stars, representing Brazil's twenty-six states and the federal district of Brasília. The stars are arranged in the constellations that were visible in the night sky on November 15, 1889—the Day of the Republic. A white banner across the sphere proclaims the motto *"Ordem e Progresso"* ("Order and Progress").

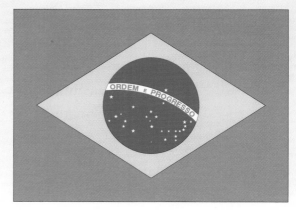

Fernando Henrique Cardoso

Fernando Henrique Cardoso (1931–) won the 1994 presidential election on the first ballot. He took office on January 1, 1995. Cardoso had previously served as minister of the economy and held posts on many state and national committees. As a professor of social sciences, Cardoso has lectured at universities around the world.

The president and vice president must be Brazilian-born and at least thirty-five years old. Voters elect both officers to four-year terms. If no candidate receives more than 50 percent of the votes, the top two candidates run in a second round of elections.

The president appoints cabinet ministers who give advice in special areas such as foreign affairs, labor, and the economy. More advice comes from the Council of the Republic and the National Defense Council. These groups are made up of the vice president, congressional leaders, and cabinet members.

The Legislature

Lawmaking power rests in the hands of the National Congress. As in the United States and Canada, Brazil's Congress is bicameral—composed of two houses. The Senate is the upper house, and the Chamber of Deputies is the lower house. Senators must be at least thirty-five years old, while twenty-one is the minimum age for deputies. All members must be Brazilian-born.

EXECUTIVE BRANCH

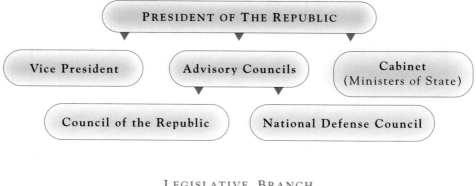

PRESIDENT OF THE REPUBLIC

Vice President

Advisory Councils

Cabinet
(Ministers of State)

Council of the Republic

National Defense Council

LEGISLATIVE BRANCH

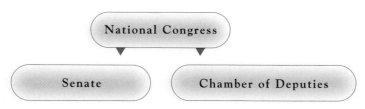

National Congress

Senate

Chamber of Deputies

JUDICIAL BRANCH

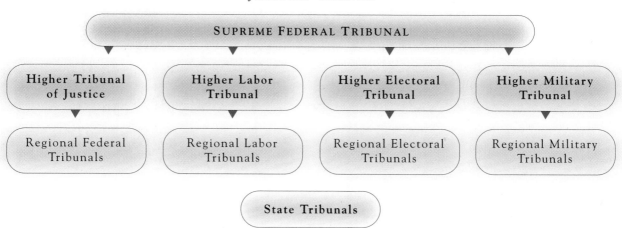

SUPREME FEDERAL TRIBUNAL

Higher Tribunal
of Justice

Higher Labor
Tribunal

Higher Electoral
Tribunal

Higher Military
Tribunal

Regional Federal
Tribunals

Regional Labor
Tribunals

Regional Electoral
Tribunals

Regional Military
Tribunals

State Tribunals

Government chart

There are eighty-one senators. Three are elected from each of the twenty-six state and the federal district. Senators serve eight-year terms. The 513 members of the Chamber of Deputies are also elected from the states and the federal district. Each area elects three or more deputies, depending on its population. Deputies serve for four years.

The Congress meets for two sessions every year. If there is a serious national problem to discuss, the president or congressional leaders may call special sessions.

The Senate and Chamber of Deputies buildings in Brasília at night

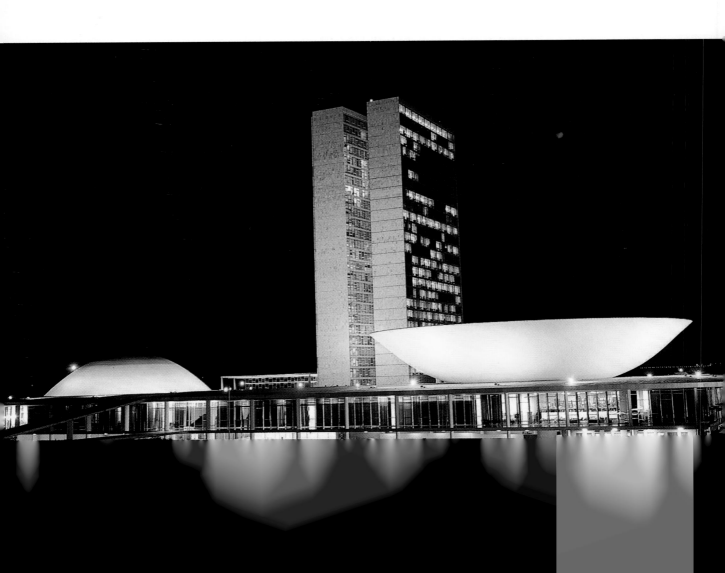

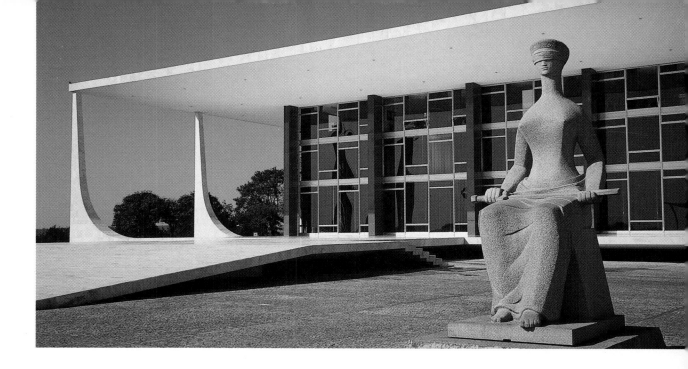

The Senate and Chamber of Deputies buildings stand side by side in the capital city of Brasília. These ultramodern buildings have been described as looking like two halves of a grapefruit. The Chamber of Deputies faces up and the Senate faces down.

The Ministry of Justice in Brasília

The Judiciary

Brazil's court system makes up the judicial branch of government. The highest court is the Supreme Federal Tribunal, which has eleven judges. As in the United States, the president appoints Supreme Court judges and the Senate approves them. These judges serve lifetime terms. Once they are appointed, they may not hold any other job.

The Supreme Court hears cases involving high government officials. It judges disputes between state courts and between federal and state courts. Supreme Court judges also rule on international lawsuits and the extradition of criminals.

Other national-level courts are the Higher Tribunal of Justice and labor, military, and electoral courts. There are regional courts in each of these categories, too. Each state has its own court system. State judges decide cases using principles set forth in the constitution.

States of Brazil

State and Local Government

Brazil is divided into twenty-six states and one federal district—the capital city of Brasília. State governments are modeled after the federal government. Voters in each state elect a governor and members of a one-house state legislature. Within each state are small regions called *municípios*, with elected mayors and municipal councils.

Political Parties

Since 1985, Brazilians have been free to organize political parties. As in other multiparty countries, the leading party changes as the citizens' priorities change. Some parties favor a strong national government, while others stand for states' rights, civil rights, or workers' rights.

In the mid-1990s, the president and the majority of Congress belonged to moderate parties. The leading groups were the Democratic Movement Party, the Liberal Front Party, and the Social Democratic Party. Other parties with strong support were the Progressive Reform, Workers', Progressive, Democratic Workers', Brazilian Workers', Liberal, and Brazilian Socialist parties.

The Military

Brazil's military has often played an important role in its government. Many Brazilian presidents have been army officers. At other times, an elected civilian president has ruled with strong military support.

Today, Brazil maintains the largest armed forces in Latin America. About 300,000 men serve in the army, navy, and air force.

The country also has a public security force of about 390,000 people. All Brazilian men are required to serve at least one year in the military. Eighteen is the youngest age for military service.

Voting Rights

In Brazil, young people have a greater voice in their government than those in many other countries. Brazilians as young as sixteen years old may vote. In the United States, voting rights begin on a person's eighteenth birthday.

By law, all Brazilians from ages eighteen to seventy who can read and write are required to vote. Lack of reading and writing skills does not bar anyone from voting, but voting is optional for people under eighteen, over seventy, or illiterate.

Brasília, the capital of Brazil, is an example of modern urban planning.

Brasília

Brasília, the capital city, stands on a plateau in Goiás state, deep in the interior. It is about 575 miles (925 km) northwest of Rio de Janeiro. Brasília was built far from major population centers in order to attract more people inland and take the crunch off the coastal cities.

Brazil's 1891 constitution called for a new federal district to replace Rio de Janeiro. Under President Juscelino Kubitschek, construction began in 1957. On April 21, 1960—Tiradentes Day—Brasília officially opened for business.

Three Brazilian designers gave Brasília its sleek, modern look: city planner Lúcio Costa, architect Oscar Niemeyer, and landscape designer Roberto Burle Marx. The city is shaped like an airplane, with government offices forming the central cabin. At the nose is the Square of the Three Powers, where the main executive, legislative, and judicial buildings are

Brasília: Did You Know This?

Population: 1.6 million (projection based on 1991 census)
Founded: April 21, 1960
Average Daily Temperature: 68°F (20°C) in July; 72°F (22°C) in January
Average Annual Rainfall: 63 inches (160 cm)
Height above Sea Level: 3,750 feet (1,143 m)

located. The airplane's wings are residential sections with high-rise apartments and businesses to serve them.

The presidential palace, called the Palace of the Dawn, stands on the shore of a V-shaped artificial lake that surrounds the city center. One of Niemeyer's masterpieces is the National Cathedral, which is shaped like a crown with angels hanging inside.

Brasília is a model of modern city design, but it has its drawbacks. As in other Brazilian cities, slums have grown up around the edges. About 1 million of the city's 1.6 million residents live in these areas. And, with few shade trees to temper the heat, residents avoid the outdoors. Some miss the vibrant cultural life of the eastern cities and escape to the coast whenever they can.

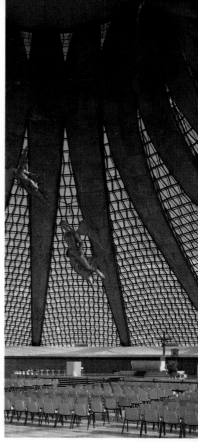

The interior of the National Cathedral, which was designed by architect Oscar Niemeyer

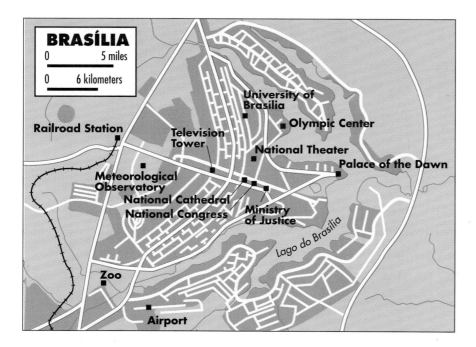

BRASÍLIA

0   5 miles
0   6 kilometers

Railroad Station

University of Brasília

Olympic Center

Television Tower

National Theater

Palace of the Dawn

Meteorological Observatory

National Cathedral

National Congress

Ministry of Justice

Lago do Brasília

Zoo

Airport

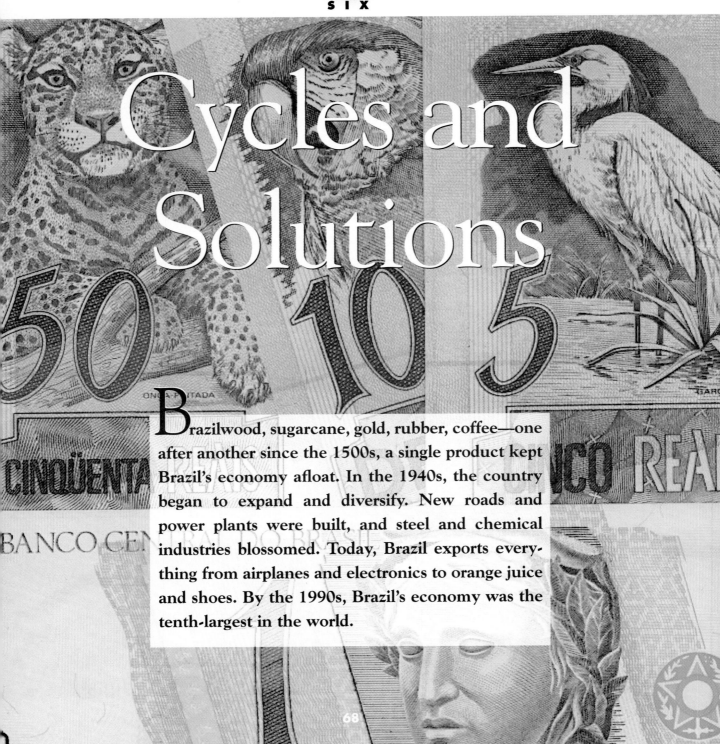

Cycles and Solutions

Brazilwood, sugarcane, gold, rubber, coffee—one after another since the 1500s, a single product kept Brazil's economy afloat. In the 1940s, the country began to expand and diversify. New roads and power plants were built, and steel and chemical industries blossomed. Today, Brazil exports everything from airplanes and electronics to orange juice and shoes. By the 1990s, Brazil's economy was the tenth-largest in the world.

B RAZIL IS A WEALTHY COUNTRY IN MANY WAYS. ITS NATURAL resources are lavish, and its gross domestic product (GDP) is one of the highest in the world. (The GDP is the value of all the products a country produces in a year—like bananas, canned food, and cars—plus the value of all the services its people provide in a year— like pumping gas, harvesting coffee, and loaning money.)

This does not mean that all Brazilians are rich, however. The wealthiest 10 percent earn half of all the income. They include high-ranking government officials and owners of large plantations, ranches, and businesses.

Trees and wood products contribute greatly to Brazil's economy. This factory produces paper pulp.

Most Brazilians live in poverty. About 20 percent of the people earn less than $120 a year. Slums called *favelas* encircle every large city. In rural areas, peasants try to eke out a living by farming or fishing. Droughts and floods are constant problems. Many people have no land at all.

Money Facts

Brazil's basic unit of currency is the *real*. Brazil has had six different currencies since 1986. The present real has been in use since July 1994.

In between the rich and the poor is Brazil's growing middle class. These are businesspeople, government workers, teachers, health-care workers, and other professionals. Over half of Brazil's labor force works in service industries.

On a national scale, the country is deeply in debt. In the 1960s and 1970s, Brazil borrowed heavily from foreign banks to help build its growing industries. Today that debt is a terrible burden. It keeps the government from spending all it would like on development projects and social programs.

Brazil is one of the leading automobile producers in the world.

Manufacturing

Brazil makes cars, trucks, and airplanes for countries all over the world. About 1.6 million motor vehicles roll off its production lines every year. Chemicals, electrical and electronic appliances, machinery, and cement are some other factory exports.

Farm products go to factories for processing, too. Various commodities end up as orange juice, raw sugar, soy meal, footwear, cotton fabric, and clothes. Palm tree cores are processed and canned as hearts-of-palm. Much of Brazil's sugarcane is distilled to make fuel.

Brazil is a world leader in manufacturing. Factory goods make up more than half of Brazil's exports to other countries. Iron and steel products are the leading manufactures—mainly because the raw materials are local and in good supply. Brazil's iron ore deposits are among the largest in the world.

Most of Brazil's factories are in São Paulo state. Rio de Janeiro, Minas Gerais, and Rio Grande do Sul states are also industrial areas. Volta Redonda's steel plant, near Rio, is the largest in Latin America.

What Brazil Grows, Makes, and Mines

Agriculture

Sugarcane	279,768,000 metric tons
Corn (maize)	32,305,000 metric tons
Soybeans	24,855,000 metric tons

Manufacturing

Motor vehicles	1,623,694 units
Tires	33,820,000 metric tons
Crude steel	25,747,000 metric tons

Mining

Limestone	58,779,000 metric tons
Crude petroleum	31,458,000 metric tons
Bauxite	9,366,000 metric tons

Brazil's traditional coffee and sugarcane plantations are bigger than ever, thanks to mechanized farming. No other country grows more of these two crops. In fact, one-fourth of the world's coffee comes from Brazil. But the days of Brazil's one-crop economy are gone forever. Brazil exports more farm products today than any country besides the United States.

Soybeans are its most valuable export crop. For the most part, they end up as cattle feed. Corn, wheat, and rice are also important grains. Cacao beans (cocoa) and cassava (manioc) are consumed locally and exported, too. One-fourth of the world's beef comes from Brazil's cattle ranches. Chickens, pigs, sheep, and goats are also raised in Brazil.

Fruits, especially tropical fruits, grow well in Brazil's climate. Brazil is the world's top supplier of oranges and papayas. Other fruits grown in Brazil include mangoes, passion fruits, pineapples, lemons, bananas, avocados, and grapes.

Coffee is one of Brazil's major farm exports.

Rubber-tapping, or extracting latex from rubber trees, provides a lot of people with their only income. Today, many forest products come from plantations instead of from rain forests. They include Brazil nuts, cashews, latex (from rubber trees), oils, waxes, gums, and resins.

Because of world demand for fine wood, the Amazon

Logs from the Amazon forest are loaded for river transportation.

forest continues to supply it. Mahogany, jacaranda, and teak are some of the major timber woods. Commercial loggers are required by law to replant, although some do not. In the southern forests, araucaria is the most important timber wood. Most is used in construction, and some is made into charcoal for fuel.

Mining

Brazil is the jewel capital of the world. There are so many jewelry stores in Brazil's big cities that the competition for business is fierce. Many jewel merchants provide cars to pick up their customers. Brazil supplies 90 percent of the world's gemstones, including diamonds, emeralds, topazes, amethysts, and aquamarines.

With its massive iron-ore deposits, Brazil exports more iron and steel than any other country in the world. Tin and bauxite (used in making aluminum) are next in importance. Brazilian mines also yield manganese, nickel, uranium, copper, lead, and gold. Deposits of niobium, found in Amazonas state in 1990, may be the largest in the world.

Petroleum (oil) and natural-gas deposits provide Brazilians with about half the oil and gas they need. From petroleum, they make petrochemicals such as fertilizer and plastic.

Most of Brazil's mines are located in the states of Mato Grosso and Minas Gerais. (Minas Gerais means "General Mines.") In the 1980s, gold discoveries in the Amazon region started a gold rush there.

Working Kids

Fourteen is the minimum age for working in Brazil. But in 1990, about 14 percent of the children between ten and thirteen years old were in the labor force. Working children in Brazil sweat their childhood away in such places as sugarcane fields, charcoal plants, and tea plantations.

Children in poor families usually start to work at around the age of ten. Their families need their wages to survive.

Mineral Resources

Al	Bauxite	Mn	Manganese
Au	Gold	Ni	Nickel
C	Coal	O	Oil
Cu	Copper	Pb	Lead
D	Diamonds	U	Uranium
Fe	Iron	Zn	Zinc

Government and industry leaders have pledged to stop child labor. They have devised plans to pay families for the income they lose when a child stops working. Still, many employers—and parents—ignore the guidelines.

Some children under the minimum age of fourteen are in the labor force. This boy works cutting sugarcane.

New Energy Sources

About 60 percent of Brazil's energy comes from renewable sources. These are resources that can be replaced, such as hydroelectricity and ethanol. Wood, the source of charcoal, is considered renewable because more trees can always be planted. (Coal, petroleum, and natural gas are nonrenewable resources. Once they are used, they are gone.)

Itaipú power plant, on the Paraná River, is the largest hydroelectric power plant in the world. It supplies electricity to homes and industries in Brazil and Paraguay. When it is operating at full capacity, the plant will provide 35 percent of Brazil's electricity. Another hydroelectric plant is Tucuruí Dam on the Tocantins River in the Amazon Basin.

Brazil produces about half the oil it needs. In the 1970s, when world oil prices rose, Brazil began to look for other, less-expensive fuels. Engineers found a solution by processing sugarcane into a fuel called ethanol.

Automobile manufacturers followed suit, developing cars that run on pure ethanol or a mixture of 80 percent ethanol and 20 percent gasoline ("80–20"). Most new cars manufactured in Brazil today use ethanol. All filling stations in Brazil offer 80–20, and most offer pure ethanol, too.

Widespread use of ethanol has cut the air pollution in Brazil's big cities. Ethanol is a cleaner fuel than gasoline. When it burns, it releases less carbon monoxide into the air.

How People Get Around

About 12 percent of the 1.1 million miles (1.8 million km) of roads and highways that crisscross Brazil are paved, while the rest have gravel or dirt surfaces. In 1995, the government launched a massive, five-year plan to improve the nation's roadways.

The southeast has a good road network for its heavy business activity. Modern expressways serve major cities such as Rio and São Paulo, and paved roads link almost all the state capitals. In the cities, buses and local rail lines provide public transportation. In rural areas, people get around on horseback.

Roads have been built in the Amazon region, but it can be risky to take them. Floodwater, potholes, shaky bridges, and the jungle make them unreliable. For example, much of the four-lane Trans-Amazon Highway—intended to run from Belém to the Peruvian border—has become overgrown with jungle vegetation.

The best way to travel into remote Amazon regions is by boat. Ocean steamers can navigate the entire length of the Amazon in Brazil. Steam-powered cargo boats chug up and down the Amazon River, carrying both cargo and people. Crew members don't bring much food along because they can catch what they need in the river. Rowboats and outboard motorboats are commonly used, too. The Indians use dugout canoes hollowed from solid logs, and even the children are experts at navigating their own canoes.

Travelers hitch a ride in São Paulo.

A container ship docked in the port of Manaus

Sixteen of Brazil's harbors are equipped to receive ocean-going container ships. The busiest ports are Santos (serving São Paulo), Rio de Janeiro, and Porto Alegre.

Brazil has a small railway system. The Steel Railway links iron mines in the interior with steel mills in southeast.

Brazil's Historic Railroad Lines

Gralha Azul ("Blue Chatterbox") runs between Curitiba and Paranaguá. The bright blue cars rattle their way through mountain gorges, tunnels, and a lush landscape of waterfalls and tropical forests.

The Devil's Railroad, in Rondônia state, took forty years to complete (1872–1912), and thousands of labor-ers died during the construction. As soon as it opened, the rubber market crashed, and the train was barely used. It has now been restored.

Maria Fumaça ("Smoking Maria"), in Rio Grande do Sul, makes a three-hour trip through mountains, vine-yards, and tunnels. Italian folk dancers perform at stops along the way.

Ten international airports operate in Brazil. Varig, the national airline, flies to cities all over the world. Smaller airlines take passengers to dozens of out-of-the-way towns.

Countless landing strips have been cleared in the forests, too. They make it easier for Indian agents, ecologists, and zoologists to do their work. On the other hand, they also make life easier for poachers, illegal prospectors, and drug smugglers.

Alberto Santos Dumont

Alberto Santos Dumont (1873–1932), a Brazilian aviation pioneer, was the first person to make and fly a gasoline-powered aircraft. Santos Dumont piloted a dirigible for 7 miles (11 km) in 1899—four years before the Wright brothers flew their first airplane. In 1906, Dumont flew his first gas-powered heavier-than-air machine.

Spreading the News

In Brazil, households with television sets outnumber those with refrigerators. Television arrived in São Paulo in 1950. Today, Brazil sends and receives programs internationally through dozens of satellite stations. Over 250 television stations and 2,900 radio stations operate in Brazil.

More than 350 daily newspapers are published in Brazil, but no newspaper reaches the whole country. It's too hard to distribute them over such a wide area. *Folha de São Paulo* has the largest circulation, followed by Rio de Janeiro's *O Globo*. Other important dailies are *O Dia* and *O Estado de São Paulo*. Rio's *Brazil Herald* is the country's only English-language newspaper. *Veja* is the nation's weekly news magazine.

Faces in the Crowd

More than half the people of South America live in Brazil. In fact, only four other countries in the world have a greater population: China, India, the United States, and Indonesia. In the late 1990s, Brazil's population was estimated at over 160 million.

E VEN WITH ALL THESE PEOPLE, MUCH of Brazil is thinly populated. That is because most Brazilians live along the coast—about four-fifths of the population live within 200 miles (320 km) of the Atlantic Ocean. By contrast, the vast Amazon region abounds in animal species but has very few of those large primates called humans. Only about 7 percent of the population live there.

Most of Brazil's big cities are near the coast, too. About three-fourths of the people live in cities, while one-fourth live in rural areas. The largest cities are in the southeast, making for another lopsided statistic: three-fourths of Brazilians live in the southern one-fourth of the country.

Life in the Cities

Almost 10 million people are packed into São Paulo, Brazil's largest city. Adding in the suburbs and favelas, the metropolitan

Persons per sq. mi.		Persons per sq. km.
more than 260		more than 100
130–260		50–100
25–130		10–50
3–25		1–10
fewer than 3		fewer than 1

Map of the population distribution in Brazil

Populations of Brazil's Largest Cities	
São Paulo	9,646,185
Rio de Janeiro	5,480,768
Salvador	2,075,273
Belo Horizonte	2,020,161
Fortaleza	1,768,637
Brasília	1,601,094

area is home to about 16 million people. That makes São Paulo the third-largest city in the world. Only Tokyo, Japan, and Mexico City, Mexico, have higher populations.

Rio de Janeiro is Brazil's second-largest city and the ninth-largest in the world. About 6 million people live in the city and about 10 million in the metropolitan area. Brasília, the capital, is one of the largest cities in the interior.

Why do rural Brazilians leave the wide-open spaces for the crowded cities? They want better jobs, housing, and living conditions. Cities also offer superior health care and nutrition. Urban residents, young and old, are healthier and live longer than rural people.

Overall, Brazilians are healthier now than ever before. In 1950, when most Brazilians lived in rural areas, the average life expectancy was forty-six years. By 1990, it had risen to sixty-five. Indians, however, do not fare so well. The average Indian can expect to live only forty-eight years.

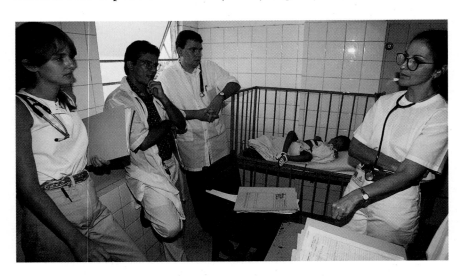

Student doctors confer at a Recife hospital. Cities offer the best health care in Brazil.

An agricultural family

Smaller Families, Longer Lives

Brazil's population has quadrupled since 1940 and is still growing—but more slowly. In 1960, the average family in Brazil had six children. Today, the average number of children is just under three. So why isn't the population shrinking?

One reason is better health care. Brazilians are living longer, and fewer infants are dying. Also, though families are smaller, more people are having children. Today, about 44 percent of Brazil's population is eighteen years old or younger. That means the number of families will continue to grow.

Historical Population Growth in Brazil

Year	Population (in millions)
1776	1.9
1876	10.9
1900	17.3
1940	41.2
1950	51.9
1960	70.1
1970	93.2
1980	121.3
1991	146.2
1995	(est.) 161.3

Who Lives in Brazil?

European Ancestry	55%
Mixed Race	39%
African Ancestry	5%
Native Indians	Less than 1%

More Japanese live in São Paulo than in any other city outside Japan.

A Multiracial Society

The mixing of races in Brazil began almost as soon as the first colonists landed. Children of Indians and whites were called *mamelucos*. Once the Africans arrived, all three races mixed to produce *cafusos*.

According to Brazil's 1991 census, about 39 percent of Brazilians are racially mixed. The primary mixed groups are *caboclos* (Indian and white) and *mulattoes* (black and white). Caboclos live in river towns and remote settlements in the Amazon. Many survive by rubber-tapping, fishing, or hunting. Mulattoes vary widely in skin shade, economic level, and self-concept. In a census survey, mulattoes described their ethnic group by fifty-three different names.

About 55 percent of Brazilians have a pure European ancestry. Most are descended from Portuguese settlers. Others are descendants of immigrants who arrived in the late 1800s and early 1900s. They came from Germany, Italy, Spain, Switzerland, Russia, Poland, and Armenia.

About 5 percent of the population are descended from African slaves. Their ancestors came from West African regions such as Yoruba (now Nigeria and Benin), Angola, and the Congo. Blacks are most numerous in northeast Brazil. About 80 percent of the people in Bahia state are black or mulatto.

More Japanese people live in São Paulo than in any other city outside of Japan. About one-half of 1 percent of the Brazilian people are Japanese. Lebanese and Syrians form another large community in São Paulo.

Brazilians say they don't understand the racial tensions in the United States. Compared to other mixed-race countries, Brazil has few racial problems and little hostility between races. Still, many Brazilians attach different social levels to various shades of skin. Also, Europeans are more likely to get a better education and therefore better jobs.

Indians

When the Portuguese arrived, there were about 5 million Indians in Brazil. Today, only about 250,000 remain—fewer than 1 percent of the population. They belong to 200 different tribes. Some of the largest groups are the Guarani, Yanomami, Tupi, and Ge.

Most Indians live in the Amazon region in protected areas set aside for them. These reserves amount to over 11 percent of Brazil's total land area. Most are in the states of Amazonas, Roraima, Pará, Rondônia, Mato Grosso, and Mato Grosso do Sul.

Even today, remote tribes who have had no contact with outsiders live by hunting, fishing, gathering, and simple farming.

Far from the city, a Yanomami mother grates cassava.

Legal Rights to Indian Lands

Brazil's 1995 Indigenous Rights Decree recognizes Indians' rights to lands that are "permanently inhabited, those utilized for their productive activities, those absolutely necessary to the preservation of environmental resources, necessary for their well-being, and those necessary for their physical and cultural reproduction, according to their customs and traditions."

It can take years for an Indian group to gain protected status, with a reserve of its own. An agent from Brazil's agency for Indian affairs—FUNAI, or Fundação Nacional do Índio—first identifies the group and applies for a ruling to go ahead. The next step is demarcation—mapping the area that the group needs for its activities. Demarcation then waits for government approval. The last step is official registration—setting aside the land for the Indians' exclusive use. In 1995, 202 Indian areas were registered, and 352 others were in earlier stages of the process.

Hand Gestures: What Does That Mean?

- Brazilians make the "come here" gesture with the palm facing down, instead of up. The fingers move with a scratching motion.
- The "thumbs up" sign works in much the same way as it does in the United States. It means, "That's great, right on, go ahead, good idea," and so on.
- Gently pulling on your earlobe means, "I really like this," or "I approve."
- Close one eyelid, lay your fingertip on it, and pull slightly downward. In Brazil this means, "Be careful," "I don't believe that," or "Are you trying to kid me?"
- Don't be offended if a Brazilian gives you the middle-finger-up sign. In Brazil, it means, "good luck!"
- Never use the "OK" sign, with thumb and forefinger making a circle. In Brazil, it's an obscene gesture.

Portuguese Pronunciation Key

This chart shows the main Portuguese letter sounds that differ from English sounds.

Letter(s)	Pronounce as	Example	Pronunciation
ç	s	moça	MOH-sah
ch	sh	acho	AH-show
g before e or i	zh	gente	ZHEN-teh
gu before e or i	g	guerra	GEH-rah*
j	zh	haja	HAH-zhah
lh	ly	filha	FEEL-yah
nh	ny	cunha	COON-yah
s between vowels	z	caso	KAH-zoh
x at the beginning of a syllable	sh	enxada	ehn-SHAH-dah

In special cases, x may be pronounced as s, ks, or z.

The above examples also show how vowels are pronounced. A vowel with a tilde (~) over it gets a nasal sound. (Practice by pinching your nose shut.) A vowel followed by m or n in the same syllable is also pronounced nasally. In those cases, the m or n is not pronounced.

*The letter r is pronounced almost like a d or a t, with the tip of the tongue lightly touching the ridge of the palate.

Common Portuguese Words and Phrases

yes	sim
no	não
please	por favor
thank you	obrigado
you're welcome	de nada
hello	olá
good-bye	adeus or tchau
How are you?	Como vai?
good	bom (masc.), boa (fem.)
so-so	mais ou menos
Where is . . . ?	Onde é . . . ?
How much?	Quanto?
What is this?	O que é isto?
Happy birthday!	Feliz aniversário!

Language

Almost all Brazilians speak Portuguese, the official language. Brazil is the only country in Latin America where Portuguese is the dominant language. The rest of Latin America is mainly Spanish-speaking. Some Brazilians also speak Spanish, English, or French. However, visitors should be prepared to communicate in Portuguese.

Brazilian Portuguese is a little different from the language spoken in Portugal—just as American English differs from British English. Several thousand Indian words and many African words also found their way into Brazil's Portuguese. The everyday, spoken language is known as *brasileiro falado*. For literary writing, a more formal version is used.

The nation's many Indian groups speak about 180 different languages. The major language family is the Tupi-Guarani. Today, Indian languages, like the Indians themselves, are "endangered species." Tupinambá, which first influenced Portuguese, is now extinct.

In the late 1980s, researchers found only two living speakers of the Xipaya language. Two speakers of Puruborá remained, too, but they hadn't spoken the language in decades.

City Problems

In the mid-1990s, there were around 3,500 favelas in Brazil. These big-city slums are overcrowded and unhealthy. People from rural areas keep pouring in every day. Many have no job skills. For housing, they set up cardboard or metal shacks. In some favelas, the government has built public housing. But most of the slums have no electricity, running water, or sewers.

Rocinha spreads across a hillside in Rio de Janeiro's southern zone. With tens of thousands of residents, it is the largest favela in Brazil. Rocinha has electricity, and some dwellings have running water. The community has its own shops and even a branch of a bank. Like most favelas, Rocinha is also a stronghold for drug dealers.

Opposite: **A favela in Rio de Janeiro**

Rio de Janeiro has increased police patrols of the city's streets (and beaches) to fight crime.

Parents who can't feed their children turn them out to fend for themselves. It has been estimated that there are 12 million *abandonados*—abandoned children—in Brazil. These homeless children sleep in alleys and doorways, begging or stealing to stay alive.

So many children and teenagers are homeless that the police sometimes target them as criminals. Merchants complain to the police about children begging outside their stores. They are afraid the beggars drive customers away. Policemen have been known to beat and even kill street children.

Street crime is another big-city problem. Gangs of young people from the slums terrorize and rob pedestrians. Pickpockets are common, too. Rio has expanded its police department to combat the growing crime. The city has also started a special "tourist police force." Officers cruise the beaches and other tourist spots in T-shirts that say "I Am Looking Out for You."

Endangered Cultures, Shattered Lives

In the 1500s, an estimated 900 Indian tribes lived in Brazil. In 1990, about 270 tribes remained. By the mid-1990s, dozens of those groups had completely disappeared too. What is happening to all the Indians?

"They're always sick," whined a settler about his forest-dwelling neighbors. White people's diseases take the biggest toll on the Indian population. Once the Indians contact outsiders, they catch diseases for which they have no resistance. Influenza, pneumonia, hepatitis, and gastrointestinal diseases are some of the biggest killers. Children under five years old account for over 40 percent of Indian deaths.

Indian reserves are meant to protect the Indians. On many reserves, however, the Indians cannot carry on their traditional ways of life. Hunters may be placed on farmland, or farmers may be living on barren soil. As a result, many Indians abandon the tribe and assimilate into white culture. Adults take menial jobs, and young people give in to the attractions of the city. In time, the tribe simply disappears.

Illegal land-grabbing whittles away at tribal lands, too. Landless peasants take land wherever they can find it. Land-hungry ranchers and plantation owners hire poor people to clear new tracts of land. Some even hire thugs to kill Indians who are in the way. Illegal logging and gold-mining are rampant.

Even legal activities endanger Indian lands. Farming, gold mining, and ranching pollutes the streams, kills off the fish supply, and makes the water undrinkable.

The Other Side

The Indian issue is not all one-sided. Landless peasants need to feed their families. Where are they to go? Timber resources are valuable to the whole country's economy. Can't they be used if they are cut in a responsible way? Many Brazilians

Yanomami Massacre

When gold was discovered on Yanomami lands in 1987, hordes of *garimpeiros* (gold prospectors) invaded the area. In 1993, prospectors murdered seventeen Yanomami Indians in order to mine on their land. It is estimated that gold hunters have wiped out 10 to 15 percent of the entire Yanomami population. Causes of death include diseases and mining pollution, as well as murder.

wonder why 11 percent of the land and its resources should belong to less than 1 percent of the people.

Indians themselves are sometimes part of the problem. One tribe, paid by land-grabbers, may raid other tribes to drive them off their land. A tribal chief may sell his own tribe's land rights for money or consumer goods.

One chief defended his land-for-goods deal with loggers: "To say Indians should stay as they are, should not have the benefits of white man's technology, is racism."

A Bororo Indian from
Mato Grosso

Miracles and Magic

Visitors to Brazil see religious symbols and practices of every kind—solemn processions with towering statues, candles glowing on the beach, flowers tossed into the ocean, a mysterious ornament dangling from an old woman's neck. Clearly, Brazilians find many ways to express their spirituality. Religious practices are yet another reflection of Brazil's cultural mix. Many people take part in the devotions and ceremonies of more than one religion.

BRAZIL HAS NO OFFICIAL RELIGION, BUT a large majority of the people say they are Roman Catholic. Portuguese priests of the Jesuit religious order brought the Catholic faith to Brazil in the 1500s. Today, there are more Catholics in Brazil than in any other country in the world.

A rural church service in Brazil

Diversity and Debates

Catholicism in Brazil is torn between two points of view. For traditional Catholics, spirituality and good works are the heart of their faith. Another trend, called liberation theology, aims to free the poor and oppressed from miserable conditions.

Liberation theology began spreading through Latin America in the 1970s. Some Catholic Church leaders oppose it because it values human efforts over divine aid. Others object because it becomes too deeply involved in politics.

Non-Catholic Christians in Brazil are growing in numbers. They include Anglicans, as well as Protestant denominations such as Lutherans, Methodists, Baptists, and Presbyterians. Evangelical Protestant groups are gaining members much faster than mainstream congregations.

Religions of Brazil

Roman Catholic	89%
Protestant	6.6%
Other*	4.4%

*Spiritism, Afro-Christian sects, etc.

Cardinal Paulo Evaristo Arns

Cardinal Paulo Evaristo Arns (1921–) was the Catholic archbishop of São Paulo from 1970 to 1996. Committed to social justice, he worked among the poor and unemployed in the favelas. Arns often clashed with Brazil's military dictators over their human rights abuses.

Evangelicals are missionaries, devoted to preaching and gaining converts. They are active in both the cities and the Amazon region. Among the Indians, their work may include translating the Bible into native languages and providing medical care. The evangelicals are also controversial. Critics say they break down the Indians' ancient cultures and speed up the disappearance of already endangered tribes.

Brazil's Japanese people practice Shinto or Buddhism. Members of the Lebanese and Syrian communities follow Islam or Maronite Catholicism. Jewish, Baha'i, and Mormon faiths are among Brazil's other religious minorities.

Candomblé

Candomblé is a religion that mixes African folk beliefs with Catholic symbols. It centers in Bahia state, where it originated among African slaves. Macumba and umbanda are variations found in other parts of the country.

Participants at a candomblé ceremony chant and dance.

The Church of Black Saints
Our Lady of the Rosary of Blacks is an eighteenth-century church in the Pelourinho neighborhood of Salvador. All the statues inside are images of black saints.

The Yoruba people of West Africa brought their ancient cults and rituals to Brazil. Portuguese slave masters banned the African practices and imposed Catholic rites. To appease their masters, the slaves "translated" their *orixás* (deities) into Catholic versions. Oxalá, god of fertility and harvests, merged with Jesus. Iemanjá, sea goddess and mother of all orixás, became Mary, the mother of Jesus. Ogum became Saint George, Xangô became Saint Jerome, and so on. Some Indian beliefs were mixed in, too.

Candomblé ceremonies often take place at night, outdoors, and near a body of water. Some are held in a *terreiro*, or spirit house. Participants arrange flowers, candles, and ritual ornaments around the ceremonial site. Accompanied by rhythmic drumbeats, they chant and dance, with some members falling into a trance.

From the African community, candomblé spread through all levels of Brazilian society. Christian churches have tried to discourage candomblé, but without much success.

Spiritism, Umbanda, and the Valley of the Dawn

Over a million Brazilians practice Spiritism, or Kardecism. They are followers of Allan Kardec, a nineteenth-century French psychic. Spiritism centers on a belief in reincarnation, mixing in some traditional Christian beliefs.

Umbanda is a religion prevalent in Rio de Janeiro. It combines candomblé, Spiritism, and other African and Brazilian folk beliefs. In contrast to the "dark" tone of candomblé, umbanda relies on "white magic." Umbandists make offerings of candles and food to their spirit protectors, who may be Catholic saints, African deities, or historical heroes. Many use magic potions to heal illness or bring love.

In a suburb of Brasília live several thousand people who expect to survive the end of the world. They belong to a religious movement called the Valley of the Dawn. Their community, with its huge temple, is also named the Valley of the Dawn.

A retired truck driver named Aunt Neiva founded the sect in 1959. She taught that a lot of ordinary people are mediums—people who can communicate with the spirit world. Mediums are easy to spot in the Valley of the Dawn—male mediums wear black shirts and the women wear long robes with star-shaped sequins.

Aunt Neiva also predicted that the world would end at the end of the millennium and that only a chosen few would survive. Residents of the Valley believe they are among the chosen. Hundreds of worshipers come into town for Sunday services. They, too, hope to prevail beyond the last days.

Religious Festivals

In Rio de Janeiro, New Year's Eve is also the umbanda feast of Iemanjá. The candlelight ritual begins at midnight. Thousands of celebrants go down to the beach, toss flowers and perfume into the waves, and make good wishes for the new year. Singing and drum-playing carry the celebration on through the night. In Bahia, Iemanjá's feast day is February 2. Revelers celebrate that day with a waterfront candomblé ceremony.

Boats gather in Bahia to celebrate the feast day of Iemanjá, the goddess of the sea.

The *festas juninas*, or June festivals, are especially popular in the northeast. They celebrate the feasts of Saint Anthony (June 13), Saint John (June 24), and Saint Peter (June 29). Festivities usually start the day before. In some regions, people make the whole month of June a festival time. Saint Anthony is honored with religious devotions, but the other feasts are occasions for fireworks, bonfires, street fairs, dances, and church bazaars.

Indian Spirituality

The Indians' religious beliefs are thousands of years old. For some tribes, spirituality is as simple as honoring their dead. Others practice complex rituals to appeal to many spirits and gods.

Most tribes have a creation myth, with a creator or a pair of creators. From the creator comes their social structure, wisdom, skills, magical herbs, and way of life. Religious practices are directed not to the creator, but to a variety of good and evil spirits. These spirits reside in animals, plants, the sun and moon, and the forces of nature.

The shaman is the tribe's religious leader and healer. He performs rites to cure illnesses, bring back lost souls, or drive out evil spirits. Often he uses medicinal herbs from the forest. An apprentice shaman may study for years to learn rituals, prayers, and incantations, as well as the healing properties of herbs.

The whole community may take part in religious dances. Adorned in body paint and elaborate costumes, they dance for hours—or even days. For some, the object is to ensure fertility

Indian Beliefs: The Yanomami, the Juruna, and the Guarani

In a Yanomami myth, Omam is the father of the tribe. One day while Omam was fishing, he caught a woman. Their children are the Yanomami people. A giant bird gathered the foam at the water's edge and formed it into the other races.

Sinaá is the mythical father of the Juruna people of the Xingu River valley. He is the guardian of a great forked stick that holds up the sky. When the last Juruna dies, Sinaá will pull down the stick. The sky will fall, and the world will come to an end.

To the Guarani, the great father Nande Ru and his family are models for human life. Family life and daily activities are living images of Nande Ru's word.

A shaman is a religious leader and healer.

or a successful hunt. For others, the dance renews their sense of who they are. It keeps them sane in a world that seems to get more and more insane.

Staying sane is not easy. In Guarani Indian communities in Mato Grosso do Sul, suicides have become almost commonplace. On their dry, weed-infested reserves, the Guarani are not able to live by their traditional hunting, fishing, and farming. Nearby towns offer alternatives. The men take jobs as common laborers, and women find work as maids. Children go to schools and want the things that town children have. Religious practices have been abandoned, and life has become meaningless.

Indian religions, like their land and their languages, are breaking down or disappearing altogether. Some Indians sell clay or wooden figures to tourists, yet have forgotten what they mean. Others go off to their factory jobs wearing feathered necklaces—relics from a lost world.

Mythical Beings

Indian spirit beliefs rubbed off on non-Indians where the two cultures came into contact. To the Indians, *cobra-grande* ("big snake") is the giant serpent of the Amazon who frightens fishermen away. The Portuguese combined this snake with the European myth of the siren. The result was the Brazilian myth of Iara, a beautiful fish-woman who entices fishermen with her haunting song.

The *curupira* is a legendary forest dweller whose feet point backward. He protects the forest from trespassers by confusing them with his backward footprints until they lose their way.

Another forest creature is the *caipora*, a hairy monster who rides a wild boar through the woods. If a hunter shoots more than one deer in a week, the *caboclinho da mata* ("little man of the forest") steals his dogs.

The boto is real. It is the pink dolphin of the Amazon River. In legend, the boto changes into a man and comes ashore to seduce women.

The *saci*, or *saci-pererê*, is a mythical fellow of the central plateaus. He is a one-legged boy with a magic red cap who hops around making mischief and scaring people.

Opposite: **A girl from a community of Asuriní Indians applies body paint to her legs in preparation for a religious dance.**

Culture and Fun

In all of Brazil, the biggest, wildest festival is Carnaval—a "last fling" before Ash Wednesday ushers in the somber, pre-Easter season of Lent. Carnaval is Brazil's version of Mardi Gras festivals in North America and Europe.

R io's Carnaval is the most spectacular. Tourists come from all over the world to enjoy the costumes, parades, flashy dancers, round-the-clock parties, and non-stop music.

At midnight on Friday the spectacle begins. All over town, people in sequins, feathers, and wild makeup jam the streets and costume balls. The samba schools' parade is the biggest attraction. Crowds pack the grandstands along the parade route to watch the floats and dancers compete for first prize.

In Salvador, the high point of Carnaval is the Electric Trio Parade. Bands on flatbed trucks put on fantastic sound-and-light shows, followed by delirious crowds.

The Puppet Parade opens Carnaval in Olinda. Puppet clubs march through the city with their 10-foot (3-m) papier-mâché puppets. Behind them marches the band, and, of course, thousands of raucous people.

Soccer and Other Sports

Brazilians love sports. They belong to about 8,000 sports clubs around the country. Most of all, Brazilians are wild about soccer.

Pelé: The World's Greatest

Edson Arantes do Nascimento (1940–), better known as Pelé, is considered the world's greatest soccer player. He led Brazil to victory in the World Cup championships of 1958, 1962, and 1970. He became the world's highest-paid athlete when he joined the New York Cosmos in 1975. Pelé began playing professionally at age fifteen and scored 1,282 goals in his eighteen-year career.

Soccer, called *futebol* in Brazil, is the national sport. Every fan knows about Pelé, Brazil's world-famous soccer star of the 1960s. Brazilians call him "The King."

Cities, towns, schools, businesses, and neighborhoods have soccer teams. Each team has its pack of wildly loyal, screaming fans. Any patch of dirt is likely to turn into a soccer field. If whites live nearby, Indians pick up soccer, too, sometimes using a coconut for a ball.

Brazil has dozens of huge soccer stadiums. Built for the 1950 World Cup soccer championship games, Maracanã Stadium in Rio is the largest in Brazil—and in the world. The stadium holds 200,000 people. During the national championships, everyday life shuts down. But the biggest match of all is the World Cup. Brazil's national soccer team won the World Cup championship four times—in 1958, 1962, 1970, and 1994.

A pickup game of soccer

With thousands of miles of seafront, millions of Brazilians take to water sports. Surfing, windsurfing, swimming, and fishing are among the favorites. Brazil has produced international champions in rowing, sailing, and swimming. Other popular sports are volleyball, basketball, hang gliding, judo, and mountain biking.

Maria Ester Bueno, the winner of the women's singles title at the 1960 Wimbledon championships

Sports Highlights

Brazil won the women's basketball world championship in 1994 and the men's basketball World Championship in 1959 and 1963. Brazil's men's volleyball team won an Olympic gold medal in 1992. Brazilian tennis star Maria Ester Bueno won the Wimbledon championship in 1959, 1960, and 1964.

In 1972, at age twenty-five, Brazilian race-car driver Emerson Fittipaldi was the youngest-ever Formula One world champion. Fittipaldi took the world championship again in 1974. Two other Brazilians have captured the Formula One world title: Nelson Piquet in 1981, 1983, and 1987; and Ayrton Senna in 1988, 1990, and 1991. Brazilians were devastated when thirty-four-year-old Senna was killed in a crash during the 1994 Italian Grand Prix.

Capoeira, a popular
Afro-Brazilian martial art

Capoeira

Capoeira is an Afro-Brazilian martial art that brings together kickboxing, acrobatics, and dance. West African slaves used it to defend themselves against Portuguese colonists. When it was banned, the slaves turned it into a ritual form and said they were just dancing.

Capoeirists use certain basic moves, but each practitioner has an individual style. In a capoeira match, the audience forms a circle around two opponents, who move to rhythmic drumbeats and heroic songs. Capoeira schools are found throughout Brazil, as well as in the United States and Europe.

Music and Dance

Thousands of sambistas sweat their spare time away in Brazil's famous samba schools. The samba, like much Brazilian music, began with African music and dance rhythms. Many different samba styles developed as Portuguese, Spanish, and pop music mixed with the African beat.

Foreigners fell in love with the samba in the 1930s. Dance bands and ballroom dancers scrambled to learn it. Rio's Carmen Miranda dazzled U.S. audiences in stage shows and movies. She did the samba in swirling skirts and a tropical-fruit headdress.

The *bossa nova* was born in Rio in the 1950s. Its father was guitarist João Gilberto, who combined jazz with cool, offbeat rhythms. Antônio Carlos Jobim launched the bossa nova craze in the United States with his hit song "The Girl from Ipanema."

MPB (*Música Popular Brasileira*) is a blend of standard pop music with Brazilian rhythms and melodies. The *lambada*, a sensual Caribbean dance, is a recent craze. The northeast is the birthplace of *frevo*, a frantic popular dance, and *forró*, a high-powered two-step. *Música sertaneja* is the folksy country music of the northeastern *sertão*.

Carmen Miranda

Carmen Miranda (1909–1955) was a singer, dancer, and actress who helped make samba popular outside Brazil. She was born Maria do Carmo Miranda da Cunha in Portugal and came to Rio de Janeiro at the age of two. After charming Brazilian audiences, she began touring the United States in 1939. Rio de Janeiro's Carmen Miranda Museum displays her costumes and other memorabilia.

Teatro Amazonas

Rubber barons built the fabulous Teatro Amazonas in Manaus in 1896. Many international opera stars sang there before it closed in the early 1900s. The ornate opera house, now restored, is open to the public. It features marble from Italy, chandeliers from France, and cast iron from Scotland.

Orchestras and soloists around the world play the works of composer Heitor Villa-Lobos. His music is based on Brazilian folk tunes and rhythms. One of his best-known pieces is "Bachianas Brasileiras."

Cordel—An Oral Tradition

Cordel, a type of folk song popular in northeastern Brazil, is a form of storytelling that grew out of Portugal's tradition of wandering troubadours. In rhyming verses, the cordel glorifies popular heroes or makes fun of political conditions. The *cantador de cordel* sings on street corners, in town plazas, and at fairs. Usually he accompanies his songs with a guitar or accordion. Most cantadores also sell printed copies of their songs.

Literature

A romantic movement called "Indianism" was popular in the 1800s. Indian themes appeared in poetry and novels, as well as music and art. José de Alancar's novel *The Guarani* became the basis for an opera by Carlos Gomes. The poet Antônio Gonçalves Dias wrote on similar subjects.

Cândido Portinari

Cândido Portinari (1903–1962) painted bold, colorful art in a unique Brazilian style. His gigantic paintings and murals can be seen in museums, public buildings, and churches. Murals by Portinari hang in the Library of Congress in Washington, D.C., and in the United Nations building in New York City.

Culture and Fun **111**

In the early 1900s, writers began to portray the harsh realities of class conflict. Euclides da Cunha's *Os Sertões* ("Rebellion in the Backlands") delves into a revolt by a group of peasants against wealthy landowners. Joaquim Machado de Assis, the son of a freed slave, wrote about Rio's high society in *Epitaph of a Small Winner*. His *Dom Casmurro* became popular all over the world.

Regional novelists appeared in the 1930s, telling of common people's folklore, traditions, and struggles. Jorge Amado wrote about his native Bahia in *Gabriela, Clove and Cinnamon*, *Dona Flor and Her Two Husbands*, and other colorful novels. João Guimarães Rosa's *The Devil to Pay in the Backlands* examined outlaw life in Minas Gerais.

Buildings, Gardens, and Sidewalks

Buildings from Brazil's colonial days look like those in Portugal. Many of them are decorated with blue-patterned ceramic tiles. Even some newer buildings are built in the colonial style, with white stucco walls and orange-tile roofs. A pattern of wavy lines in sidewalks is an old Portuguese design.

The finest colonial buildings are churches. Igreja São Francisco in Salvador glitters with gilded carvings. Here and throughout Bahia state, the artisans were slaves.

Colonial-style architecture and design, like these ceramic tiles, link present Brazil to its Portuguese past.

Opposite: **Church of São Francisco in Ouro Preto**

Minas Gerais has some of the most beautiful colonial churches, built with money from the gold boom. Churches in the town of Ouro Preto are especially ornate thanks to the mulatto sculptor Antônio Francisco Lisboa, who carved countless statues out of cedar and soapstone. (*Ouro Preto* means "black gold." Black nuggets found in the area's streams in the 1600s turned out to be gold covered with a black mineral.) Lisboa also decorated altars and church exteriors with elaborate curlicues.

Bigger cities created bigger building problems. Modern architects have tried to design buildings, neighborhoods, and cities that are both useful and artistic. Affonso Reidy designed low-income housing outside of Rio, as well as Rio's Museum of Modern Art.

The public buildings in Brasília are the best-known examples of modern Brazilian architecture. The architect, Oscar Niemeyer, also built the Church of Pampulha in Belo Horizonte and helped design the United Nations headquarters in New York City.

Brazil's cityscapes of concrete and steel are softened by lush gardens and parks. Many are the work of Roberto Burle Marx, Brazil's world-famous landscape designer. Burle Marx was also a botanist who collected the native Brazilian plant species that grace his gardens and landscapes.

Sônia Braga—From Sesame Street to the Silver Screen

Sônia Braga (1950–) was born in Maringá, Paraná, and began acting at fourteen. Children first saw her on Brazil's *Sesame Street* show. Today, she is a TV and movie actress. Among her credits are *The Cosby Show* and several movies, including the comedy *Moon over Parador*.

Local Crafts

Salvador's waterfront market is packed with artisans' stalls. They offer jewelry, wood carvings, hammocks, native musical instruments, and Afro-Brazilian voodoo charms. Caruaru, in Pernambuco state, is the scene of a twice-a-week craft fair.

Salvador is full of crafts shops like this one.

Brightly painted ceramic figures of monsters and mythical creatures are among the most popular items. Shoes, bags, belts, and other leather goods are specialties in ranching regions.

Craftsmen around the São Francisco River are known for their *carrancas*. These are cedarwood carvings of frightful, half-man, half-beast figures. Fishermen used to affix them to their boats as figureheads to scare off evil water spirits.

Soapstone is quarried near Ouro Preto, where sculptor Antônio Francisco Lisboa lived and worked. Today, sculptors in the region make soapstone figures in many shapes and styles. Some carve modern designs, while others imitate Lisboa's techniques.

Indians make baskets with mythical figures woven into the designs. Their necklaces and bracelets are made of bird feathers or animal teeth. Clay and wooden figures represent tribal deities.

Slices of Life

A recent *Veja* magazine survey asked Brazilians how they think of themselves. About 84 percent said they are more hospitable than people from other countries.

It's true that Brazilians welcome others—literally—with open arms. "Hello" and "good-bye" come with handshakes or, among friends, hugs. Women greet each other with kisses on both cheeks. An unmarried woman gets a third kiss for good luck in finding a mate. When Brazilians chat, they often stand close and physically touch each other.

116

VISITORS FROM OTHER COUNTRIES don't always understand these customs. They may feel that Brazilians are "invading their space," making advances, or pledging eternal friendship. But to the Brazilians, these are just casual ways to express their natural warmth.

Family Ties

Family ties in Brazil are strong. An extended family of three or more generations stays close, often living in the same home. Brazilians trust their family members and count on them for friendship and support. Holidays are times for huge family get-togethers, and most leisure time is spent with family members.

Relatives are often chosen to be a child's godparents. If the godparents are not related, they are often treated as part of the family. If something happens to a parent, godparents take the children in and care for them as their own.

Family ties in Brazil are strong.

Dating and Beyond

Young people begin dating in groups at around age fifteen or sixteen. This gives them a chance to get to know lots of other people in a low-pressure setting. In time, they may break off into individual couples. A two- or three-year engagement before marriage is not unusual.

A student in a village school

Traditionally, courtship followed rather formal rules. When a couple was ready for serious dating, the boyfriend asked permission from the girl's father. At some point, the couple became officially engaged. That, too, called for a sweaty session with the future father-in-law. Today, however, more young couples are making their own dating decisions, without consulting their parents first.

Education and Literacy

Free public education is available from preprimary through university level. Children from ages seven through fourteen are required to attend school. Many drop out after that, and a great number of children never go to school at all. In 1991, only 16 percent of high-school-age children were enrolled in school.

High-school programs last three years, from age fifteen through seventeen. There are two types of high school in Brazil. Academic schools prepare students for college, while vocational schools lead directly to jobs. Many of Brazil's high schools are private Catholic institutions.

Brazil has over 120 colleges and universities. About 70 of them are state supported, and most of the others are Catholic schools. The University of Rio de Janeiro is Brazil's oldest university, and the University of São Paulo is its largest. Students take entry exams to get into a university, whether it is public or private.

Brazil's literacy rate has risen dramatically in the last half-century. In 1950, about 50 percent of Brazilian adults could read and write. By 1995, literacy had risen to 83 percent. Literacy is highest in the southeast and lowest in the northeast.

Students at the University of Rio

National Holidays in Brazil

New Year's Day	January 1
Carnaval	four days before Ash Wednesday
Good Friday and Easter	
Tiradentes Day	April 21
Labor Day	May 1
Corpus Christi	May or June
Independence Day	September 7
Our Lady of Aparecida	October 12
All Souls' Day	November 2
Day of the Republic (also Election Day)	November 15
Christmas	December 25
New Year's Eve	December 31

In the Cities

City life in Brazil moves at breakneck speed. The traffic can be terrifying. It's said that normally laid-back Brazilians go wild once they get behind the wheel. High-speed taxi drivers whip around anything in their path. Yellow lights are invitations to step on the gas.

In Rio de Janeiro, as in other coastal cities, the beaches are jammed with sunbathers, soccer players, and snack stalls. Skimpy bikinis are the rule for women and girls. Nightlife is serious business. Dinner and dancing start late and can easily last all night. In São Paulo, life is more geared to business and industry. Culture, entertainment, and faces in the crowds reflect dozens of nationalities.

Residents of São Paulo are called "Paulistas," and the people of Rio de Janeiro are called "Cariocas." To show the difference between the two cities, Brazilians like to quip: "Paulistas work, while Cariocas play."

Home life often revolves around family meals—and television. *Telenovelas*—nighttime soap operas—begin at 5 P.M. and go on for hours. They're so popular that people schedule their activities around their favorite shows.

Keeping Time

Brazil spans four time zones. The far-western state of Acre, in the Amazon, has its own time zone. When it's noon in Acre, it's also noon in New York City. At the same time, it's 1 P.M. in Manaus (Amazon Time) and 2 P.M. in Rio de Janeiro (Brazilian Standard Time). On the tiny islands off the coast, it's 3 P.M.

Opposite: **Rio de Janeiro's beaches are packed with sunbathers.**

Shops usually stay open from 8 A.M. to 6 P.M. on weekdays and 8 A.M. to noon on Saturdays. Some businesses close from noon till 2 P.M. for a long lunch break. Lunch (*almoço*) is served between 11:30 A.M. and 3 P.M. Dinner (*jantar*) is late—7 to 11 P.M. Café colonial is the afternoon coffee break.

Brazilians keep time on the twenty-four-hour clock. For example, three o'clock in the afternoon is 15:00.

Brazilian cuisine is a combination of ethnic and regional foods.

A World of Food Choices

Indian, African, and Portuguese food meet on the dinner tables of Brazil. Each region and ethnic group has its distinct flavors. Meat, rice, and black beans are basic ingredients, along with fresh fruits and vegetables.

Feijoada, a meat and bean stew, is the national dish. Lunch is the time for feijoada, and Saturday is the day to eat it. At home, Brazilians fuss over their preparations and invite guests over for hours of eating. Some restaurants fix huge pots of feijoada and serve it all day long.

West Africans gave Brazilian food its spicy flavors and its big-pot style. Slaves had a "cooking-pot" tradition, tossing leftovers and local produce into a big pot on the fire. As cooks for plantation owners, they flavored their dishes with traditional African foods—coconut milk, dendê palm oil, and peppers.

African influence is strongest in the foods of Bahia. Specialties include *vatapá* (shrimp, fish, dendê palm oil, and coconut milk); *saratapel* (pig's liver and heart, tomatoes, peppers, and onions); and *carurú* (shrimp, okra, and red pepper sauce). In the open-air markets, Bahian women in flowing dresses cook *acarajé* (deep-fried fish cakes) in big pots.

Churrasco is the regional favorite in the south. It is made of beef chunks grilled on 3-foot (91-cm) skewers. Out on the range, gaúchos make churrasco by roasting an entire steer over a fire pit. In the *churrascarias* (churrasco restaurants) of Rio Grande do Sul, the food comes with a stage show of local song and dance.

Bahian women cook deep-fried fish cakes called *acarajé* at a Salvador market.

From the Indians came sweet potatoes, hearts-of-palm, manioc, and chocolate. Indians also taught the Portuguese how to preserve meat by drying and smoking it. In the Amazon region, some choice dishes are *pato no tucupi* (duck in a hot, green-herb sauce) and *tacacá* (yellow shrimp-and-garlic soup).

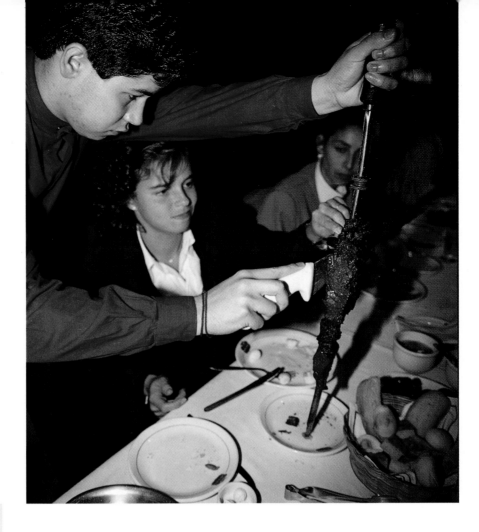

A churrasco restaurant in Rio de Janeiro

Know Your Food Names

bread	*pão*
coffee	*café*
dessert	*sobremesa*
fish	*peixe*
fruit	*fruta*
meat	*carne*
salad	*salada*
tea	*chá*
vegetables	*legumes*
water	*água*

The Portuguese brought food traditions to Brazil, too. Their coffee, syrupy desserts, and dried fruits came from the North African Moors who once occupied Portugal and Spain. In Brazil, colonists made the same foods, only with local ingredients. Brazilian desserts include angel's belly (egg yolks and sugar), angel's chin (syrup-coated tarts), maiden's drool (coconut pudding), kisses of a farmer's daughter (coconut cakes), and mother-in-law's eyes (prunes stuffed with coconut paste).

Immigrants added another layer of food choices. Germans brought schnitzel, sausages, and strudel. The Japanese brought sushi (raw fish), and Spaniards brought paella (a seafood stew).

Brazilians drink *cafezinho* (strong black coffee), *café com leite* (coffee with milk), or a tea called *maté*. There are tropical fruit juices galore. An Amazon fruit called *guaraná* is made into a popular soft drink. The national cocktail, *caipirinha*, is made with sugar, crushed limes, and sugarcane extract.

Brazilians—and people around the world—drink a local beer made by Amazon Indians. They brew beer by fermenting manioc, maize (corn), sweet potatoes, and other plants. Honey often provides the sugar needed for fermentation.

A Place to Call Home

Middle-class Brazilians rent apartments in high-rise buildings or own houses in the suburbs. The upper class lives in elegant condos or palacelike homes. Some have high iron fences and armed guards to protect themselves and their property.

In startling contrast are the favelas on the hillsides behind Rio. They look right down on luxury condos and hotels. Favelas have spread far beyond the city centers. In most of them, living conditions are dangerous or unhealthy. Houses in some favelas are built on stilts over streams of sewage. Those on hillsides are in danger of being washed away by landslides. Still, many longtime residents take pride in their homes, keep them neat, and paint them bright colors.

Table Manners
Brazilians eat "continental style," with the fork in the left hand and the knife in the right. Even pizza and chicken are eaten with a knife and fork. Both hands should always stay above the table, but the elbows should never rest on it. Brazilians stay seated until they're finished. They never eat while walking or driving.

In the rural northeast, home is a one- or two-room house made of adobe or stone with a tile roof. Near rivers and swamps, houses are built on high poles. Ranch and plantation owners live in rambling houses with wide, covered porches.

Indians build shelters of sapling trunks or cane stalks. Roofs are made of palm branches. "Furniture" is a hammock strung between poles. Some tribes live in villages of thatched-roof huts built in a circle around a central area.

Malocas, in the northwest Amazon, are large, round communal houses, some with more than 100 residents. Each family has its own space, though there are no inside walls. The Indians don't need walls to separate themselves from each other. Mutual respect is all they need to make a place to call home.

Opposite: **A family from Belém on their dock**

Timeline

Brazil's History

The Treaty of Tordesillas divides the Americas between Spain and Portugal.	1494
Pedro Cabral discovers Brazil and claims it for Portugal.	1500
Rio de Janiero is founded.	1565
Spain rules Portugal and its empire, including Brazil.	1580–1640
Gold is discovered in Minas Gerais.	1695

World History

c. 2500 B.C.	Egyptians build the Pyramids and Sphinx in Giza.	
563 B.C.	Buddha is born in India.	
A.D. 313	The Roman emperor Constantine recognizes Christianity.	
610	The prophet Muhammad begins preaching a new religion called Islam.	
1054	The Eastern (Orthodox) and Western (Roman) Churches break apart.	
1066	William the Conqueror defeats the English in the Battle of Hastings.	
1095	Pope Urban II proclaims the First Crusade.	
1215	King John seals the Magna Carta.	
1300s	The Renaissance begins in Italy.	
1347	The Black Death sweeps through Europe.	
1453	Ottoman Turks capture Constantinople, conquering the Byzantine Empire.	
1492	Columbus arrives in North America.	
1500s	The Reformation leads to the birth of Protestantism.	

Brazil's History

Portugal and Spain sign the Treaty of Ildefonso.	1777
First major rebellion against Portugal's rule is led by Tiradentes.	1789
Napoleon invades Portugal, forcing Dom João to flee to Brazil.	1807
Dom João names his empire the Kingdom of Portugal and Brazil.	1815
Brazil proclaims independence from Portugal.	1822
Slavery is abolished in Brazil.	1888
Brazil becomes a republic.	1891
Brazil declares war on Germany during World War I.	1917
The "Old" Republic ends; the "Vargas era" begins.	1930
Brazil declares war on Germany and Japan.	1942
The Vargas era ends.	1954
The capital of Brazil is moved to the new city of Brasília.	1960
Twenty years of military dictatorship begins.	1964
Free and open elections mark the return of democracy in Brazil.	1985
A new democratic constitution is adopted.	1988

World History

1776	The Declaration of Independence is signed.
1789	The French Revolution begins.
1865	The American Civil War ends.
1914	World War I breaks out.
1917	The Bolshevik Revolution brings Communism to Russia.
1929	Worldwide economic depression begins.
1939	World War II begins, following the German invasion of Poland.
1957	The Vietnam War starts.
1989	The Berlin Wall is torn down, as Communism crumbles in Eastern Europe.
1996	Bill Clinton is reelected U.S. president.

Fast Facts

Official name: Federative Republic of Brazil

Capital: Brasília

Official language: Portuguese

Official religion: None

Flag of Brazil

Founding date:	1822, independence from Portugal; November 15, 1889, birth of the republic; 1988, present constitution
Founder:	Dom João IV of Portugal
National anthem:	"*Ouviram do Ipiranga*" ("The Peaceful Banks of the Ipiranga")
Government:	Multiparty federal republic with two legislative houses
Chief of state:	President
Head of government:	President
Area:	3,286,486 square miles (8,511,992 sq km)
Dimensions:	north-south, 2,684 miles (4,319 km) east-west, 2,689 miles (4,328 km)
Bordering countries:	Brazil borders ten South American countries: French Guiana, Suriname, Guyana, Venezuela, Colombia, Peru, Bolivia, Paraguay, Argentina, and Uruguay. (Chile and Ecuador are the only South American countries that do not border Brazil.)
Highest elevation:	Pico da Neblina, 9,888 feet (3,014 m)
Lowest elevation:	Sea level

Average temperatures:	in July	in January
Brasília:	68°F (20°C)	72°F (22°C)
São Paulo:	60°F (16°C)	73°F (23°C)

Average annual rainfall:	
Brasília	63 inches (160 cm)
Western Amazon	160 inches (406 cm)
Northeast interior	10 inches (25 cm)

National population: 161,382,000 (1995 est.)

Population of largest cities in Brazil:
(projection based on 1991 census)

São Paulo	9,646,185
Rio de Janeiro	5,480,768
Salvador	2,075,273
Belo Horizonte	2,020,161
Fortaleza	1,768,637
Brasília	1,601,094

Famous landmarks:
▶ Amazon rain forest (in the northeast interior)
▶ Itaipú Dam, the largest dam in the world (on the Paraná River)
▶ Sugar Loaf Mountain and Christ the Redeemer statue (in Rio de Janeiro)
▶ Federal capital buildings and cathedral designed by Oscar Niemeyer (in Brasília)

Industry: Service industries make up about three-fifths of Brazil's gross domestic product (GDP). They include government, education, health care, retail trade, and many other services. Manufacturing, mining, and construction industries account for another 31 percent of Brazil's GDP. Most of that is manufacturing. Cars, iron and steel, and food are the major products. Agriculture, forestry, and fishing make up 9 percent of Brazil's production. Coffee and soybeans are the most important crops.

Currency: Brazil's basic unit of currency is the *real*. 1997 exchange rate: U.S.$1=0.95 real

Weights and measures: Metric system

Literacy: 83.3%

Common Portuguese Words and Phrases:

adeus or *tchau*	good-bye
boa (feminine)	
bom (masculine)	good
Como vai?	How are you?
de nada	you're welcome
Legal!	Cool!
mais ou menos	so-so
não	no
O que é isto?	What is this?
obrigado	thank you
olá	hello
Onde é . . . ?	Where is . . . ?
por favor	please
Quanto?	How much?
Que legal!	Awesome!
sim	yes
Tri-legal!	Excellent!

To Find Out More

Nonfiction

▶ Bender, Evelyn. *Brazil*. New York: Chelsea House, 1990.

▶ Carpenter, Mark. *Brazil: An Awakening Giant*. New York: Macmillan, 1988.

▶ Lerner Geography Department Staff. *Brazil in Pictures*. Minneapolis: Lerner Publications, 1987.

▶ Lourie, Peter. *Amazon: A Young Reader's Look at the Last Frontier*. Honesdale, PA: Caroline House, 1991.

▶ Reynolds, Jan. *Amazon: Vanishing Cultures*. New York: Harcourt Brace, 1993.

▶ Richard, Christopher. *Brazil*. Tarrytown, NY: Marshall Cavendish, 1991.

▶ Siy, Amanda. *The Amazon Rainforest*. New York: Macmillan, 1992.

Videotapes

▶ *The Brazil Experience: Northeast.* Lonely Planet, 1995.

▶ *The Burning Season.* HBO Movies, 1994. The story of Chico Mendes and his struggle to save his native forestland.

▶ *The Emerald Forest.* Embassy Pictures, 1985. Based on the true story of a North American boy who grew up among an Amazon Indian tribe.

▶ *Fitzcarraldo.* New World Pictures, 1982. The story of an opera lover determined to build an opera house as grand as the one in Manaus.

Websites

▶ **Capybara Home Page**

http://www.access.digex.net/~rboucher/ capybara/
Provides pictures, habitat description, zoos that have capybaras, and links to other capybara and animal sites.

▶ **Rainforest Action Network**

http://www.ran.org/ran/
Provides a wealth of information on the Amazon and other rain forests around the world. Includes a Kids' Corner, with steps you can take to save the rain forests.

▶ **Information Services of the Brazilian Embassy**

http://www.cr-df.rnp.br/brasemb/ washington/embing6.htm
Provides a news log, travel tips, and information about Brazil's government and scientific research.

▶ **International WWW School Registry**

http://web66.coled.umn.edu/schools.html
Links to home pages of K-12 schools in Brazil and all over the world.

Organizations and Embassies

▶ **Brazilian Embassy**

3006 Massachusetts Avenue NW
Washington, DC 20008
(202) 238-2700

▶ **Brazilian-American Chamber of Commerce**

22 West 48th Street, Suite 404
New York, NY 10036
(212) 575-9030

Index

Page numbers in *italics* indicate
illustrations

Meet the Author

Ann Heinrichs fell in love with faraway places while reading Doctor Dolittle books as a child. She has traveled through most of the United States, several countries in Europe, Morocco, the Middle East, and east Asia. Her travels in Portugal provided a background in the language, history, and arts of Brazil.

"Trips are fun, but the real work—tracking down all the factual information for a book—begins at the library. I head straight for the reference department. My favorite resources include United Nations publications, world almanacs, and the library's computer databases.

"For this book, I also read sixteenth-century explorers' journals, current Brazilian news stories, and anthropologists' studies of Amazon Indians. The Internet was a super research tool, too. I found everything from Brazilian Embassy facts and figures to daily soccer match results."

"To me, writing nonfiction is a bigger challenge than writing fiction. With nonfiction, you can't just dream something up; everything has to be researched. I study government reports, analyze statistics tables, then try to give the information a human face. And I'm always looking for what kids in the other country are up to, so I can report back to kids here."

Ann Heinrichs grew up in Arkansas and lives in Chicago. She is the author of more than twenty books for children and young adults on American, Asian, and African history and culture. (*Tibet*, in the first Enchantment of the World series, was awarded honorable mention by the National Federation of Press Women.) Ann Heinrichs has also written numerous newspaper, magazine, and encyclopedia articles. She holds a bachelor's and master's degree in piano performance. These days, her performing arts are tái chi, nan chuan, and kung fu sword.

Photo Credits

Photographs ©:

Archive Photos: 44, 47, 51
Archive Photos/Popperfoto: 107
Chip and Rosa Maria de la Cueva Peterson: 48, 84
Comstock: 13, 45, 120, 131
Corbis-Bettmann: 50, 109
Erwin C. "Bud" Neilsen/Images International: 117, 118
Gamma-Liaison: 77 (Ricardo Beliel), 90 (A. Sassaki), 114 (Randi Leigh Sidman), 60 (Diana Walker), 40
Mary Altier: 126, 127
North Wind Picture Archives: 46, 49, 52
Panos Pictures: 15, 19, 72 (Maria Luiza M. Carvalho), 73, 113 (Michael Harvey), 10 (John Miles), 75, 83 (Paul Smith), 82 (Jon Spaul), 43, 95, 99, 133 (Sean Sprague)
Photo Researchers: 122 (David Frazier), 36 top (Dan Guravich), 39 (Ken M. Highfill), 32 (Tom Hott), 41, 94, 96 bottom (Jacques Jangoux), 119 (Bobbie Kingsley), 110 (Will & Deni McIntyre), 8, 9, 12, 33 bottom, 85, 130 (Leonide Principe), 7 bottom, 33 top, 37 (Jany Sauvanet), 70, 78 (Ulrike Welsch)
Reuters/Corbis-Bettmann: 106 top
Robert Fried: 106 bottom
Superstock, Inc.: 21, 23, 66, 67, 80, 92, 115
Tony Stone Images: 34 (Ary Diesendruck), 89, 132 (David Frazier), 58, 62, 63, 97, 108, 116, 123 (Sylvain Grandadam), 7 center, 16, 17, 26, 29, 36 bottom, 102 (Jacques Jangoux) 25, cover, spine, cover, 6, 7 top, 22 bottom, 31 (Will & Deni McIntyre), 112 (Suzanne Murphy), 27 (Donald Nausbaum), 69, 101 (Martin Rogers), 2 (Joel Simon), 104 (John Starr), 38 (Gary Vestal), 35 (Art Wolfe), 22 top
UPI/Corbis-Bettmann: 54, 55, 79, 96 top, 111
Vanderlei Almeida/Reuters/Archive Photos: 56
Visuals Unlimited: 124 (Jeff Greenberg).
Maps by Joe LeMonnier